A QUESTION OF TRUST

A QUESTION OF TRUST

A CEO's Guide to Effective Communications and Trust-building

GAYATRI RATH

PAARUL CHAND

MACMILLAN

First published in India 2020 by Macmillan
an imprint of Pan Macmillan Publishing India Private Limited
707, Kailash Building
26 K. G. Marg, New Delhi 110 00
www.panmacmillan.co.in

Pan Macmillan, 6 Briset St, Farringdon, London EC1M 5NR
Associated companies throughout the world
www.panmacmillan.com

ISBN 978-93-89104-00-4

1 3 5 7 9 8 6 4 2

Typeset in Guardi LT Std by R. Ajith Kumar, New Delhi
Printed and bound in India by Replika Press Pvt. Ltd.

This book is dedicated to the many communications professionals who work tirelessly behind the scenes to relay the voices of CEOs to their stakeholders.

CONTENTS

FOREWORD

ARE WE GOING THROUGH the biggest crisis of the last 100 years or are we on the threshold of unimaginable opportunities that may be within our reach if we are willing to stretch ourselves? The answer to the question lies in communication backed by intent and what it is that we want the foreseeable future to be.

On the one hand, there's a massive slowdown in growth – a global phenomenon – and on the other, the kind of technology adoption and instantaneous innovation that we have experienced leaves us with tremendous hope of what lies ahead. In the last six months, digital adoption for many people and industries have amplified ten times over or even more. This contactless world which we have entered is here to stay, and we aren't going back to the old ways, when face-to-face interaction was taken for granted.

The offshoot of this great change is a data-driven, trust-led economy that is hard to build but easily lost if the standards aren't met.

Communication is the most important tool in a leader's kit. There are two parts to it – internal and external. In times of crisis, especially a prolonged one, the toll on people can be heavy. All the solutions to it may not be forthcoming and that's perfectly normal – but it's *not* okay to pretend that the problems don't exist. On the contrary, people appreciate it hugely if communication is open and honest. The process of arriving at a solution to an unnamed problem is evolutionary, and leaders must not shy away from saying, 'I don't know right now, but as a team, we will get there.'

The stress test for effective communication is the action that follows immediately after. Actions, and timely ones at that, need to follow the words if one has to lead in a trust-led environment.

External stakeholders comprise customers, the government, business partners, vendors and the community at large. Almost everyone today is facing challenging circumstances and trying hard to sustain and build on existing relationships. When growth is uncertain, organizations look to cost as the controllable lever and that does not always leave a favourable impression. Be that as it may, for the first time, many big budget deals are being conducted virtually and without the reassurance of the customary handshake. That's the level of trust people are showing one another.

The corporate communications team is a company's brand custodian and has to be alert as to what's happening externally and position the brand accordingly. With multiple channels, the format is never uniform, and yet the tone and tenor cannot be compromised. While leaders struggle to get revenue back in order, inappropriate communication can set things back further – more than one can imagine.

This crisis must not be allowed to go waste and the Indian technology sector understands this very well. It's an opportunity to reimagine and reinvent who we are, what a brand stands for, and sustain communication in a way that addresses these angles most effectively.

Given this backdrop and the deep interlinkages that exist, I am extremely happy to write this foreword to *A Question of Trust*, the timeliness of which the authors must be congratulated for. The importance of communication will reach an altogether different level in the new normal, and this book deftly explains its significance by distilling the cumulative learnings of some of the leading lights of our industry.

Debjani Ghosh

September 2020 — President, NASSCOM

INTRODUCTION

A Question of Trust: Why the CEO Urgently Needs a Comprehensive Communications Strategy

ONE THING THAT THE 2019 Indian general elections and the 2020 pandemic have proven in spades is that people, not newspapers or television or digital platforms, are the new media.

The Covid-19 pandemic specifically made the communications distance between a CEO and their people (employees, customers, peers) extremely short. A mere tweet is enough to get the attention of and access to a CEO. This is an unprecedented situation and a challenge for the CEO of any firm: to be available and accessible at all times, reasonable or not, and to respond, solve, guide and inform about whatever issue the CEO is being asked to comment on.

This change in communications is permanent. If you look at the role of the CEO pre-Covid-19 era, it was to grow, manage and inspire the company's team members to perform so as to meet the business goals of the organization. It remained, especially in cultures like South Asia, fairly patriarchal and highly centralized. The startup boom in the region a decade ago and the attention given to 'rockstar CEOs' of startups further emphasized that the role of the CEO in India and South Asia remained similar to that of the head of the family, with access and communication controlled accordingly.

A political example of this style of CEO leadership is also seen in Prime Minister Narendra Modi and the BJP's entire brand communications strategy to get 'CEO' Modi elected in 2019. The strategy was around direct interaction with the 'customers', that is, the voters, bypassing the mainstream media – which were the traditional carriers of communication by leaders. In this way, Modi controlled how he communicated and how he was perceived.

He was able to successfully do so also because he was also willing to use 'enrage and engage' as a communications strategy and expand the window of negative issues that could be talked about in the public domain.[1] It did not matter that a group of people who are labelled as 'elite liberals' hated this approach and voted against him. The vast majority loved it and voted for him.

This was also observed in the recent clashes with China and his handling of the pandemic. His appearance at the border provided a great photo opportunity with the troops, allowing him to strike a commanding pose, quite in the manner of a king posing on the fort ramparts to inspire his subjects. His addresses to the nation with regard to the pandemic were also in the manner of a head of the family or patriarch laying down the new rules for the household. But what works for an elected leader does not work for a corporate CEO. Especially in the post-pandemic era.

The modern CEO cannot take this approach without risking a negative impact on his personal and the company's brand image. The CEO cannot ignore, let alone enrage, a customer, a partner or a policy influencer group. He needs to empathize with, connect to and inspire each one of these groups. They cannot leave any group behind. CEOs are increasingly being called upon to perform the role of the 'chief trust officer' for their organizations.

A CEO today, therefore, needs to be able to communicate effectively with several audience groups, way beyond the immediate customer of their product or service. The audiences include the government, employees, peers, customers, potential customers and market influencers – both at home and in international markets. If you consider the range of these audiences, it seems like a daunting task. One that is over and above the main purpose of a CEO: to deliver business results.

The Post-pandemic CEO: Inclusive, Clear-headed, Trustworthy and Inspiring

The post-pandemic CEO needs to show strong leadership. But strong in ways that includes and inspires, lays down the vision and gets the buy-in of all the stakeholders: employees and employers, customers and non-customers. It is all about building circles of trust with all these different audiences, with communication providing the means to do so. It is a delicate balance that is achieved by communicating correctly.

The CEO needs to deal with several generations in the course of a day, from his peers to middle management to young professionals who need to be inspired more than others. The leadership of many firms during the pandemic have made special efforts to reach out to their young colleagues, especially if they are staying alone or with ageing parents, even going to the extent of planning their household rations for them and calling their extended families. It is leadership with good interpersonal and communication skills that have made this extra effort to inspire and reach out.

In the pre-pandemic era, rockstar CEOs, who were highly visible but perhaps not empathetic or vulnerable, could thrive and did. However, Covid-19 has changed all of that. A recent article by *Fast Company* lists confidence–resolve, perseverance and being vulnerable as three of the most important CEO traits during a crisis such as the pandemic.[2].

Management gurus, such as Jim Collins, have shared research that shows startup CEOs underperform compared to CEOs who are more reticent.[3] At the same time, it is rare to meet a CEO who cannot sell and talk about the company's products. By definition, the role of the CEO is externally focused. Startup CEOs are especially externally focused on brand communications as the survival of the brand is at stake as they offer a product or service that needs to be talked about.

It is the quality, tone and content of a CEO's communication that defines their effectiveness. And that is more important than ever in these difficult times.

Why this Book will Work for You

A Question of Trust is aimed at helping CEOs and corporate professionals be strategic in terms of planning messages for their target audiences, prioritizing who they should be talking to and who can wait, and how to ensure that the CEO is smartly engaged with the tidal ebb and flow of the feedback available today.

CEOs should expect their corporate communications teams to help them in several areas:

1. Listen better, to all stakeholders, and make sense of the overflow of information from multiple sources.
2. Develop strong and clear messages that articulate the position of their organization.
3. Drive branding, for themselves and their organizations.
4. Be good spokespersons.
5. Drive an inclusive organizational culture.

All of the above goals are in sync with certain qualities the modern CEO is expected to possess. This book discusses ways to obtain the best audience feedback in an age where correct information is gold; to articulate and share their vision clearly and then carry the team along towards that goal; to be a brand ambassador for the company – the truest and the most authentic one; and to ensure employees are engaged and motivated, especially during a crisis such as the pandemic.

If any of these goals resonate with you – with respect to how one needs to communicate in a corporate world: strategically and with measurable impact – then this book is for you.

With close to five decades of combined experience in news reporting, news analysis, public relations and corporate communications, the book's authors Paarul Chand and Gayatri Rath have observed and worked closely with hundreds of communications stakeholders: CEOs, cross-sections of business leaders, politicians, think tanks and leaders in the non-profit sector. The chapters in this book draw from this range of experiences as well as recent interviews with a group of experts and contributors.

You may ask why a book on something that should come naturally; certainly communication is being human! The reason is the sheer scale and frequency of modern communications and its impact on CEOs and brands. Communications is a corporate function that is as important to a company's business as sales or marketing. Yet, many firms tend to bypass and ignore this important function. Having worked in communications throughout their careers, Paarul and Gayatri hope to share their learnings about the role and impact of communications on a brand, a business and how it can be one of the most important tools for effective leadership for the post-pandemic CEO.

This book is for both the CEO of an established firm, who wishes to fine-tune and maximize their business impact using communications, and the startup CEO or entrepreneur who wants to learn how to use communications as a growth hack for their company. Through the chapters of this book, readers can understand how to set up and implement the full range of communication strategies for companies – from setting up listening posts to listening to key audiences to managing crises.

The book is packed with interviews with current CEOs and global corporate communications heads representing a wide range of sectors. In the subsequent chapters, the reader will meet Suresh Narayanan, Chairman and Managing Director of Nestlé India, who shares his take on how communications fits into the overall matrix of a company. He also shares his experience with communications when he returned to India during the Maggi-crisis in 2014.

D. Shivakumar, former CEO of Pepsi and currently Group Executive President of Corporate Strategy and Business Development, Aditya Birla Management Corporation, gives tips on how he manages communications as a corporate leader.

Dave Samson, former General Manager, Public Affairs at Chevron and part of the Arthur W. Page Society's Hall of Fame, speaks about how to manage communications for a wide range of stakeholders including local communities.

Paarul and Gayatri believe that branding and communications professionals the world over are embracing new learnings and adapting to meet the demands of a new information-driven world. The role of communications professionals has changed from being guardians of information flow to strategic advisors who help organizations build trust. Even if you are not a CEO and wish to build your personal brand, this book can help you with a personal branding roadmap. Young professionals today, who have grown up in the Industry 4.0 information-driven age, are especially open to learning the best way to brand themselves. These young professionals do not like to wait till they have reached a senior management or CEO role to communicate and build their professional brand and create personal impact. They are already talking about their work, life and company via blogs, tweets, Instagram posts and WhatsApp. This book will be useful for them too.

The forthcoming chapters will help the reader discover how to use corporate communications to drive their brand, its business objectives and broader important goals, such as driving inclusiveness. It also provides suggestions that will help CEOs and corporate professionals set up the right corporate communications department suited to their needs, to develop their priorities in terms of communications as well as measure the impact of their communications, especially during a crisis. It also explains how to be an effective spokesperson. The examples and tips in the book's chapters are drawn from the authors' first-hand experiences in relevant fields.

I

HISTORY AND POSITION OF CORPORATE COMMUNICATIONS

1

RISE OF THE CORPORATE COMMUNICATIONS DEPARTMENT

Mass Media and Unidirectional Communciation

IT WOULD NOT BE wrong to say that the advent of organized mass media gave birth to modern corporate communications. Mass media gave a platform for discussion and discourse outside the pillars of modern society – government, citizens and the law. With mass media, for the first time in human history, people had a platform that potentially rivalled the reach and influence of a religious group or a political structure. Users of mass media – like, corporations – required structured communications outreach to fully utilize the power of the platform.

Several world events were responsible in shaping the corporate communications function as we know it today. The growth of modern journalism in the early nineteenth century fueled a need to manage the flow of information from an organization to its customers and partners. With the two

World Wars and increased awareness about public health in the 1950s and 1960s – with regard to polio, tobacco and cancer – people around the world demanded greater and more transparent information about policies and products that impacted their lives. Corporations needed to manage the flow of information to their shareholders and customers. Meanwhile, the rise of popular television in the western world presented a megaphone that was more effective than any street corner or town hall promotion.

Over time, corporations moved from regulating the flow of information to deliberately shaping perceptions. For over fifty years, starting in the 1950s, reputation management was at the core of the corporate communications function. The American automotive industry excelled at it. After the Korean War of 1950, the American automotive industry used media relations to fight what they labelled as excessive government taxation by highlighting that cars were a necessity and not a luxury item[1]. Many successful global industries used communications as a powerful tool to lobby for favourable policies in the 1960s, 1970s and 1990s. The trend continues to this day, albeit with more nuance.

The Internet and Multidirectional Communication

In the 1990s, things changed significantly with the coming of the commercial Internet. The Internet disrupted the way organizations communicated with their customers, partners or employees. The Internet media impacted traditional media and news reporting as well. Corporate communications was no longer a source of unidirectional information outreach and dissemination. Multidimensional platforms and channels sprung up to help organizations reach informed and discerning users.

In a conversation with us, Dave Samson, former General Manager of Public Affairs at Chevron and a global communications industry veteran for thirty years, said, 'Most communications departments were built in the analog world. Today we are moving in a digital world, an AI world, a cognitive world. In the new world, people come together based on shared experiences, shared belief and shared interests.'[2] He explained that experiences and emotions connect people more than geography, ethnicity or company.

The Internet has changed the way traditional organizations interact with their audiences. Something the pizza company Domino's found out in 2009. Two disgruntled employees posted a video online of unhygienic practices during the pizza preparation process. The video soon went viral.[3] The *New York Times* quoted a Domino's spokesperson Tim McIntyre, and reported that the company was preparing a civil lawsuit against the truant employees. McIntyre said, 'Even people who've been with us as loyal customers for 10, 15, 20 years, people are second-guessing their relationship with Domino's, and that's not fair.'

By the mid-2000s, the Internet had started to impact work cultures within the organizations. Business leaders had started to feel the need to communicate faster and more transparently with their employees, customers and partners. Employees connected and collaborated more with one another. With the advent of social media – starting with Orkut and LinkedIn and followed by Facebook a few years later – the role of the corporate communicator further evolved. However, not all the Internet trends survived. One example of this is Second Life, for brand communication. Second Life is a platform where people and brands can create their avatar in a virtual world. It is a parallel make-believe universe that allows engagement with employees and other audiences. IBM owned twelve islands on Second Life at one time. In 2006, the company generated terrific media hype by holding a block party on the platform.[4] But IBM has since moved out of Second Life.[5]

***

The Covid-19 pandemic is arguably the biggest world event that has affected us in recent times. The pandemic is a great example of how widespread communciations have kept people aware and connected. In mid-April 2020, according to an estimate by a global newspaper, one-third of the global population was in lockdown. Through these unprecedented times, communication was an important tool used by governments around the world. New York City Mayor Andrew Cuomo held a daily public brieifng. Indian Prime Minister Narendra Modi addressed citizens directly through live video streaming three times in a single month. Information from the World Health Organization and national health bodies was shared every second of the day through Internet-based chat and social media platforms. People who were otherwise uninterested in scientific advancements, kept track of ongoing research to find a vaccine for Covid-19. The role of communciations professionals during this crisis was less about the dissemination of information and more about helping people process the information overload and ascertain what was necessary to keep themselves healthy and safe. In other words, not just communicating but shaping the assimilation and processing of a desired communication impact the pandemic has irrevocably established the significance of corporate communciations.

The evolution of the modern corporate communications department can be categorized into three phases. The first phase was about managing relations with the media and, by extension, with the public. The second phase was about reputation management when organizations tried to shape perceptions by deliberately communicating in a certain manner, and the third phase – currently underway – is marked by the need, for risk management and trust-building with respect to social and political issues.

Shaping Industry Norms

In the 2000s, against the backdrop of growing Internet usage, global corporate communications departments evolved to manage a firm's interactions with society and governments. This is truer for industries with disruptive technologies like Internet-based companies or those in transportation or new energy solutions areas such as Uber, Tesla and Facebook. New-age consumer companies, such as Facebook and Uber, and Microsoft and Google before them, have created strong outreach programmes to influence national laws and policies.

Often, new-age companies, like ride-sharing and co-working space companies, operate in areas that do not have clear societal and business norms or defined government regulations. For instance, is driver welfare Uber's responsibility or not? As these organizations create highly successful commercial businesses, they self-regulate (or are expected to self-regulate) to create credibility for themselves and their industries. This is not unlike what newly formed banks and financial institutions in the eighteenth century encountered. Today's new businesses need to help governments and social organizations create balanced frameworks to guide the responsible growth in their industry. CEOs and their communications partners need to address trust and credibility challenges faced by their organizations.

Corporate Communications in India and South Asia

Professional corporate communications is a relatively new management area in India and South Asia. PR consultancies began offering professional services in the 1990s. In those days, many consultancies operated solely to drive positive media coverage for their clients. There was the occasional campaign that went the extra mile, but oftentimes both the client and agency were happy to return to the world of counting positive media stories. Any consultancy promising bigger, better positive media stories was sought after. Those early years were before the dawn of the Internet. PR executives spent hours printing press releases on dot matrix printers and then distributed them by hand. Later, in the early 2000s, mass faxing was introduced. A national news dissemination exercise needed advance planning. If an organization wanted to make an all-India announcement, they would print and post the press release through an overnight courier on the previous day. There was no fear of news leaks via courier intercepts.

In the early 1990s, foreign multinationals started establishing their presence in India, bringing with them western public relations practices. The rise of business journalism amplified the need for professional communicators within a commercial organization.

Pepsi's entry into India was preceded by a national debate about allowing foreign companies to operate in the country, in sectors that had been out of bounds so far. The debate lasted four years and took up much political and government mind space. A total of 250 questions were raised in the Indian Parliament and thousands of media stories were written for and against the venture between the years 1986 and 1990.[6] Then came the economic liberalization of India in 1991. Pepsi and several other storied entries of Western brands into India in the 1990s set the ball rolling for professional public relations services as well as its main counterpart, business journalism, in the country. It also set the ground rules for professional relationships between business journalists and professional PR practitioners.

Soon PR and media professionals were sought after to run in-house communications departments for global brands. These companies inevitably brought in their communications practices. Over the years, the in-house corporate communicators in South Asia developed their own practices to suit the needs of local audiences. Gradually, local best practices emerged from local experiments.

There were various other changes taking place in the Indian subcontinent during the late 1990s. Television news was booming, the Internet had entered the workplace and after the dotcom explosion, South Asian dotcoms seemed as aggressive and ambitious as the Silicon Valley ones. The clamour for funding and valuation was evident and gave rise to a sharp increase in the demand for communications services. The rise of the information technology services industry in India and South Asia changed the way people looked at career growth and stock options. It also changed how the media regarded corporate governance practices – giving rise to the need by greater transparency and disclosure for organizations.

From Public Relations to Corporate Communications

The corporate communicator's role is no longer about managing the media or informing certain sections of the public. It is about managing the organization's link with its various audiences to create trust and belonging. There are three realities that have helped reshape the role of corporate communicators in South Asia:

1. Internet-based communication platforms have made information sharing much more democratic, with 90 per cent of 600 million[7] Indian Internet users are on one or more platforms such as Facebook, WhatsApp and TikTok (until it got banned). With 290 million users on Facebook, India is Facebook's largest market.

2. Audiences no longer have to be masses that consume information passively – they can now participate in an exchange as aware, discerning and opinionated individuals. And they demand personal communications tailored to their unique relationship with the organization or brand.
3. Who doesn't love a well-told story? Consumer to CXOs, people want to hear things that move them. In fact, if you study any successful election campaign, you will notice how politicians and community leaders use this to their advantage. Often, powerful stories have the potential to polarize public opinions.

Authenticity is the cornerstone of the modern corporate communications department. In their book *Marketing 4.0*, Philip Kotler and his co-authors write about the role of 'expressive evangelists' on the Internet and their role in telling authentic stories from the point of view of customers.[8] Corporate ccommunications departments are now using these third-party 'expressive evangelists' to tell their stories, using voices that promote trust in their company and brand.

As the modern corporate communications department have evolved, so have professionals working in these departments and the processes followed by them. Corporate communicators have learnt (or are learning) to create and measure trust, brand credibility and meaningful brand relationships. Corporate communications departments are now setting up a trust barometer[9] for their organization.

2

COMMUNICATIONS OR MARKETING?

COMMUNICATIONS IS A RELATIVELY new management field. Over the last century it has made a place for itself in boardrooms and within leadership structures. Sometimes, however, communications is confused with marketing. At other times, it is treated as an extension of marketing. On multiple occasions, we have heard CEOs ask whether they should invest in communications or marketing.

The confusion between communications and marketing functions arises from an overlap in the audiences both address and the channels they use to reach them. In simplistic terms, both help connect a company's products with their users. Both functions convey the value of a product, a service or an idea to its core audiences. Both employ mass media and online outreach tools to drive customer engagement. The two functions, however, are dissimilar in many ways. They have different goals.

Marketing focuses on growing sales and the top-line, while communications involves creating the right environment and equity to support that growth. Communications focuses on building trust over increasing consumption and buying. Unlike in marketing, people in communications departments do not measure their success through the lens of monthly product sales. For them, success is measured in terms of stakeholder perception audits and trust levels of audiences. More importantly, communications builds connections with the organization's entire ecosystem including its most ardent critics which may be civil society, think tanks, media and analysts.

The CEOs we interviewed while writing this book agreed that organizations need both communications and marketing. They play unique and, at times, somewhat overlapping roles in the success of an organization. Drawing from forty years of management experience, Bhaskar Pramanik, the former Chairman of Microsoft India, said that the relative importance of marketing or communications is usually a function of whether the company in question is a product or services company; a startup or a mature company; or if the industry is a highly regulated or unregulated one.

Many companies are reinventing themselves and re-evaluating their purpose and mission as doing more than just maximizing return to shareholders' growth and earnings. There is a greater realization that a company's purpose must add value to the community, nation, or the world. For such companies, communications plays a critical role in ensuring that the entire organization, customers as well as other stakeholders are energized.

D. Shivakumar, another seasoned business leader in South Asia, who has led brands such as Nokia and Pepsi, believes different industries use communications and marketing differently. In his opinion, technology product companies such as Microsoft, Oracle and Salesforce use integrated marketing and communications to drive understanding and demand for new technologies. For these companies, communications programmes may also have goals like driving sales targets, something consumer goods industries may not do.

Suresh Narayanan, long-time business head and the Chairman and Managing Director of Nestlé India, said that trust is at the centre of the relationship with a consumer. Marketing is an 'operational connectivity' between a brand and its consumers, and the role of communications is to 'build neural connectivity'. Narayanan narrates stories of mothers calling the Nestlé call centre in India to ask nutrition-related questions when planning their children's diet. He cites this as a clear demonstration of their trust in the brand, the result of a successful communications program.

According to Vicky Bindra, a tenured global business leader in the financial services industry, everything in business has to do with communications. Speaking with us in an interview, he said, 'How you interact with your customer, partners or industry peers is defined by the company's communications strategy. Any marketing a company chooses to do is a subset of that overall communications strategy.'

Our experience shows that successful CEOs, while balancing their investments in both marketing and communications, lead with communications in specific situations. These are usually times when they need their stakeholders to connect and engage with the company instead of just buying a product. Such scenarios may include:

1. When an organization wants to **define or redefine their position** vis-à-vis their industry or in the context of society, as Microsoft did in 2014 under their new CEO, Satya Nadella.
2. When an organization needs to **increase trust,** as Facebook realized in the face of data privacy concerns, or Uber did just before their initial public offering.
3. When an organization needs to **manage a crisis better,** as Nestlé India did when they had to deal with the Maggi ban in India.

Defining the Position of an Organization

Organizations which define themselves clearly – who they are, and what they stand for – can convey their vision and mission with confidence. They are able to inspire others – employees, partners, shareholders and investors – to join their journey. The process and journey for defining a vision and a mission may vary from organization to organization. The CEO is the curator of that journey.

For newly formed organizations, it is both easy and difficult. It is easy to define their position in their industry or society as there is little baggage of failed products, processes or customer relationships weighing them down. At the same time, it can be difficult as the company's business direction may not be clear right at the beginning. Numerous and conflicting market opportunities may pull the organization in many different directions, thus diluting its priority list.

Even established organizations struggle with their priority list. Microsoft found itself in a similar situation in early 2014. The company had lost the phone and apps battle to Android and seemed unsure about the future of its traditional business areas. Employee morale was down as well. The new CEO Satya Nadella asked: 'What will the world miss if Microsoft disappeared?' This was the beginning of a soul-searching exercise that involved speaking with and listening to hundreds of employees, customers and partners. In 2015, the company adopted a new mission statement: 'To empower every individual and organization on the planet to achieve more.'[1] Nadella personally wrote a letter to his employees to explain the new mission.[2] It helped sharply focus Microsoft's various overlapping and, at times conflicting, business groups. The new mission gave employees, customers and partners new energy and a new purpose. The mission was supported by a new business strategy as well. That was the starting point of a transformation in the company. Microsoft went on to become the most valuable company in the world in 2019 with over a trillion dollars in market capitalization.

To give another example, in 2018, a twenty-year-old fintech company in India that was reasonably successful in its niche, wanted to accelerate its growth. Their CEO asked his company the following question: 'Who are we and what makes us different from others in the market?' A three-month dialogue involving the leadership, employees and many customers and partners led to the formulation of the organization's vision and mission statements. They found a clear articulation of their raison d'être – make merchants successful. A little over a year later, the company crossed the $ 1 billion valuation threshold.

In these scenarios, communications was the catalyst for change. The communications team can help the leadership team focus on what is important. Listening and speaking with both internal and external stakeholders, using structured communications workshops and distilling varied opinions can help leadership teams acquire a strong sense of purpose that can guide them through the next phase of growth.

Increasing Trust

Organizations today deal with more aware and informed people than ever. According to the United Nations, more than ninety per cent of the people in the world had attended school and received some form of education by 2017. About half of the world's population has access to the Internet and consumes global content. This means people know what they want and what they like. Megaphonic advertising is losing its appeal with these audiences. Users and consumers do not want to be sold to; they want to have the freedom to choose and decide themselves.

In 2002, Al and Laura Ries wrote in their book *The Fall of Advertising & Rise of PR*, 'No matter how creative the advertising, no matter how appropriate the medium, there is just no way around the issue of credibility.'[3] Credibility and authenticity are guiding brand custodians to rethink how they connect with their stakeholders – customers, partners, employees, investors and industry opinion leaders. Brands are investing in owned digital storytelling platforms.[4]

Authentic voices are now preferred over actors. Uber used its drivers to convey its impact on jobs and the community in the run-up to its initial public offering in mid-2019. They followed it up with a driver-led campaign to accelerate business in the aftermath of the Covid-19 lockdown. Customers and partners are the preferred voices for storytelling. GE Reports,[5] the Microsoft News Center[6] and Flipkart Stories[7] are such examples of owned platforms that tell an organization's story in an authentic, believable and engaging voice. The stories of real people evoke real emotions in readers, viewers and listeners. They build trust.

Managing Crisis

Crisis tests trust in a brand. In 2016, the 150-year-old Indian business conglomerate, Tata Group, faced questions about the manner in which their then chairman, Cyrus Mistry, was ousted. They responded with full-page advertisements, aggressively defending their board's decision. This was perhaps one of those rare occasions when the Tata Group advertised aggressively on any topic, leave alone a sensitive governance issue.

In another example, Facebook wanted to introduce Free Basics in India, an initiative that sought to bring Internet access to first-time Internet users by giving them free access to specific services from Facebook and its consortium. Campaigns against it by anti-monopoly voices, including a digital and telecom news website *MediaNama*, made it a national public debate. As the regulator deliberated on whether to allow Free Basics in India or not, Facebook reportedly spent $ 40 million on advertisements in leading media outlets, espousing the benefits of the initiatives and urging the regulator and its own users in India to support it. The regulator ruled against Free Basics. Facebook had to shelve its India plan for Free Basics. A well-organized and credible anti-Free Basics campaign had won. Yet, a similar initiative in several African countries has brought digital and financial inclusion to remotely located communities.

In both these examples, the organizations used public platforms to aggressively put forth their point of view. And yet, they failed to break through to their core audiences. A more nuanced approach may have, perhaps, worked better. At times, subtle messaging through authentic voices trumps witty television commercials or direct front-page advertisements.

Communicators, owing to their access to external points of view, many of which are highly critical of the company, have a much more balanced approach to managing crisis. As the CEO's role extends to those of chief engagement officer, chief empathy officer and chief empowerment officer, they need to have both marketing and communications in their arsenal. They may choose communications when they need to build trust among their expanded group of stakeholders as 181 United States CEOs pledged in the 2019 Purpose of Corporation Declaration.[8]

II

COMMUNICATIONS AND THE CEO'S ROLE

3

CEO'S ROLE #1: LISTEN WELL

IN EARLY 2019, FACEBOOK tested a new dating-like feature within their app. It was perhaps a response to Bumble and Tinder, two dating apps that seemed to be gaining popularity at that time. Later in the year, Facebook officially launched the feature for its users.[1] Companies have elaborate research mechanisms to understand product feedback and user preferences. They use these to improve their products or introduce new products. These mechanisms however may not work as well in keeping CEOs updated on the preferences and sentiments of their other stakeholder groups, such as employees, investors, shareholders, suppliers, distributors and regulators. There are other groups of stakeholders that are important too. For CEOs of IT product companies, the developer community is of key importance while CEOs of ridesharing and food delivery companies need to understand their service delivery partners, such as drivers and delivery agents.

A lack of proper listening mechanisms can thus sometimes result in misreading public sentiment or employee sentiment.

According to Echo Listening, a US-based consultancy, businesses lose billions of dollars – $ 62 billion – due to poor listening.

Maggi, the more-than-century-old noodle brand from Nestlé, was banned in India in 2015 following allegations of lead in its seasoning. In a conversation, a senior Nestlé India executive told us that after they faced this crisis, they expanded the consumer services team and further enhanced their listening mechanisms. [2]

During the two World Wars, both the German army and the Allies had extensive networks of listening posts to crack the enemy code. These posts warned of imminent attacks and helped strategists assess the strengths and weaknesses of the enemy campaign. At one such listening post in England, Alan Turing's work led to the Turing machine that has now evolved into what is widely known as artificial intelligence.[3] Just like the listening posts that helped the troops on both sides during the World Wars, listening posts in business can help CEOs read the pulse of their organization, markets and competition.

Business leaders, boards and CEOs require information channels that are efficient and effective. When an organization is undergoing change in its business direction or culture, or is facing a crisis, these information channels become invaluable.

These channels must:

1. communicate good and bad news equally well;
2. relay information fast; and
3. transmit news and information in the right context without distortions and unnecessary embellishments.

Setting Up Listening Posts

Each organization can devise its own listening posts. The communications team can work with the CEO and the leadership to decide what works best for their organization. These listening posts may include surveys, blogs, discussion boards and chats on digital collaboration tools. Social media platforms are also a reliable channel for listening and for audience sentiment analysis.

Other listening mechanisms could be an annual employee satisfaction and sentiment survey, a periodic analysis of feedback from the service centre or customer care centre or structured conversation with partners and customers. Organizations may use a brand value framework to listen to their key stakeholders.

In 2016 and 2017, Microsoft's CEO Satya Nadella addressed a monthly employee town hall that was open to all 1,00,000 employees globally.[4] For employees who could not attend it live, it was recorded and posted on the employee portal. In an interview with us, Shiv Shivakumar, an experienced CEO, vouches for the monthly employee town hall. While at Nokia and Pepsi, he used it as a mode of open communication with employees and found it useful in curbing rumours and gossip. It proved especially effective during periods of organizational change.

Unstructured listening posts can be equally valuable. Informal conversations with employees in the cafeteria or in the elevator could provide a peek into employee sentiment about a new initiative. Sometimes, CEOs may devise their own unstructured communications channels. Shivakumar sent mobile text messages to employees in his organization after each monthly employee town hall to gauge their mood.

Designing Listening Posts with UX

Google, Facebook and Zoom have painstakingly built products by listening to and analyzing user preferences. User experience, or UX as it is known now, is a strong new discipline that intersects with communications and marketing in many places. Be it the size of the entertainment screen in aircrafts, the colour or shape of the icon on a phone app or the angle at which the kickstand on a tablet opens, UX touches every aspect of our lives. The science of building user-friendly products can be extended into other areas of management. One of these is how CEOs listen to their core stakeholder groups. CEOs can integrate UX into their listening in order to connect with, and respond to, their stakeholders. For example, take the case of the enterprise chat solution you choose to implement. An easy mobile app-based enterprise chat solution can help CEOs connect quickly and easily with their field sales teams and receive feedback and suggestions in real time rather than waiting for days or weeks before the information travels up to them through more traditional communications routes. The lack of such a tool forces employees to rely on sending an email or speaking up at an employee all-hands meeting, neither of which are good options, as psychologists will tell you.

Listening during Crisis

When the Covid-19 pandemic broke out, governments and companies struggled to keep their employees safe while keeping the business going. The crisis was compounded by the lack of information about how the disease could spread, how the infection could be effectively contained and for how long people had to be quarantined before they could be declared infection-free. In the early days, a great deal of time on the Internet was spent debating whether N-95 masks or common surgical masks were effective. Many countries reported an acute shortage of N-95 masks, even for medical professionals, as the panic-stricken public began to hoard these items. A crisis may arise from an unforeseen development that may be physical (an oil spill), regulatory (government banning a service or product) or market-related (the global financial crisis of 2008) or customer preference (the shift in from on-premise products to cloud-based IT products) or medical (Covid-19, SARS).

A crisis is a period of insecurity for employees, partners and customers. During a crisis, facts sometimes get lost in a blur of emotions. At such times, understanding what stakeholders are thinking, feeling or experiencing, and responding appropriately to such reactions, can make an organization stronger. Conversely, these situations can make an organization weaker in the event of a bad response to a crisis. When organizations find themselves in a crisis, the listening posts need to become hyper-efficient. The listening posts need to be imbued with integrity, resilience and scalability to meet the demands of a fast-changing situation.

Connecting the Dots

It is not enough to set up listening posts and collect information, feedback and suggestions. An organization must have a mechanism to respond quickly and appropriately to what it is hearing.

Extracting information out of half a dozen sentiment reports, perception audits and customer survey, and helping the CEO and leadership team see the trends is part of the communications team's job. Good communicators are entrenched inside an organization. They have friends in every department. They know when the next big product milestone can be achieved, and what customers love or hate about their company. A well-established communications team can sense a dip in stakeholder sentiment or rising excitement among employees before it shows up as a question at the shareholder meetings or all-employee meetings. Working with external audiences gives communicators the opportunity to hear feedback and suggestions from critics such as media, analysts and pressure groups.

The art and science of listening is evolving. CEOs will often find themselves facing a deluge of information daily, and it is imperative that they decide what information to trust, process and then act upon. Thoughtfully developed listening mechanisms could well be the difference between the success and failure of a strategy.

4

CEO'S ROLE #2: MESSAGE CLEARLY

When the Boss Talks the Walk

ACTION IS WHAT TYPICALLY defines a CEO and his role. A CEO, by necessity and also, quite often, by personality, is very focused on the delivery of the business goals of their organization. And these business goals require the CEO to concentrate on a wide range of activities: these could be around operations, supply chain concerns (a big issue in the post-Covid-19 world for companies manufacturing products), sales, marketing and managing the operating environment of the firm.

Where does communication usually fit in for a CEO? It is a tool to convey the various action points that need to be implemented day in and day out.

In fact, a large organization is like a mini nation with the CEO having to take dozens of decisions every day for the 'citizens'. The CEO, of course, recognizes very well that what needs to be done has to be communicated, via emails, meetings, video conferences, phone calls, operating manuals and other channels.

But a CEO who understands the value of communication for itself substantially elevates the potential of the business, the company and the brand. How, one may very well ask.

When we asked Vani Kola, Managing Director of Kalaari Capital, how important communication is when it comes to one's role as the CEO, she said, 'The CEO's job is to create alignment on vision, goals and values.'[1] Different CEOs have their unique style of communicating. She spoke of how Reed Hastings of Netflix used a 107-slide presentation to convey the company's values.

Kola added, 'Some are great writers. I tend to write a lot, but that's just the way I have trained myself: to be clear about what I want to say. Some may be better orators or design a silent incentive system about what the [company's] values are. I think: formal, informal. One shouldn't be prescriptive about these. What doesn't work is to expect anyone [stakeholder] to be a mind reader.'

She also narrated a famous management anecdote about how Mr Marriot would visit his hotels incognito to assess them and leave as quietly as he came. Then he wrote long memos to the manager of that hotel on what he observed during his visits. That, according to Kola, is a form of aligning stakeholders to the values of the organization.

When D. Shivakumar first joined PepsiCo in India, he made it a point to hold what in effect are 'pop-up' town halls. Typically, town halls, which are meant to be a platform for employees and interested stakeholders, are organized on a large scale. Very often they are also stage-managed with set questions. Shivakumar decided to do away with such town halls and pre-decided questions. He worked with his communications team and prepared a new style of town halls, in effect a new style of communication. They moved between office sites talking, interacting, listening and communicating. In another example, in the wake of a major brand crisis for a food multinational in India, the new CEO and India chairman went on walkabouts in the office interacting with employees.

Amazon's Jeff Bezos is another great example of a CEO who communicates strategically during the 'big bang' moments. On his visit to India in January 2020, dressed up in an Amazon Basics sleeveless Nehru jacket, hands folded in a namaste, he looked the part even before one heard him speak. He went on to announce a massive billion-dollar investment (via a blog) to assist the digitization of small businesses and creation of one million jobs. With a word in praise of Mahatma Gandhi, he also declared that the twenty-first century belonged to India. A town hall was held at Delhi's Jawaharlal Nehru Stadium. The communication outreach was evidently planned in detail, and his message was clear and precise.

The reason Bezos' India communication was impactful was because he communicated strategically, rather than through reaction.[2] He did not react to the negative responses of central government ministers to his investment announcement that preceeded his appearance. Rather he stuck to his communications playbook by keeping the reigns of external interactions in his hands. Much like Anand Mahindra who also controls his communications by using Twitter as his primary channel of communication and maintaining a regular flow of comments on a wide range of issues. But the content shared is always meaningful, never flippant. Communication is an integral part of crisis management, and CEOs often go into communication mode as the crisis unfolds. While this is a step in the right direction, if one has not created a clear communication plan and built appropriate channels and platforms in advance, it is unlikely that the crisis communication will be as effective as expected.

Define Your Thoughts and Message

For an apt illustration of the need for planned communication, we turn to the *Asterix* comics. (We recommend comic books such as *Peanuts*, *Asterix* and *Calvin and Hobbes* for some insightful lessons in communications. For a more obvious corporate-themed read, there's always *Dilbert*.)

Asterix and Obelix have to earn a cauldron full of sestertii (an ancient Roman coin) to replace the one stolen under their guard in the little Gaulish village. They try their hands at freestyle theatre, and Obelix is not given any lines and asked to perform impromptu by the long-haired director. A frightened Obelix mutters, 'But what about the message?' The hand is pointed, the cue is given and a shaking Obelix, suffering from stage-fright, looks at an audience full of rich Romans and says, 'These Romans are crazy!' All hell breaks loose. Asterix and

Obelix are thrown into prison. Later in the story, they break out of the prison, and the unrepentant director has a date with the lions at Circus Maximus.

As the story suggests, the message does not just materialize on the spur of the moment. It must be both well planned and well practiced, and delivered just at the right time to create the maximum positive impact.

Crystallizing One's Message

The Obelix anecdote has several lessons for CEOs and the C-suite in general who face audiences regularly. Here is a quick checklist on how to deliver strong messages.

1. Be clear about your company's goals, objectives and values. Why does your company exist? How does it interact with the world around it? What is the company's vision and mission, and what are its organizational values?
2. Be true to the DNA of the brand. Look into the very reason for the existence of your brand. The message has to flow from here. To quote an old Hindi saying, '*Bata ka joota aur Tata ki naukri*' (shoes from Bata and a job with Tata) echoes the values of a Bata product and Tata as an organization. Both were symbols of stability, longevity, reliability and a certain sturdiness.

   Let's look at a less obvious example of product values: the family refrigerator. The basic theme of the messaging around most of these devices is the same: keeping the food fresh, highlighting features such as the particular placement of the chill tray or the vegetables compartment. Along with these product-based specifications, a strong sense of family and togetherness is also conveyed. The communication doesn't deviate much from this. Let's consider a service-based example: OTT platforms such as Skype, WhatsApp and Netflix. Here too, the messaging is around the features: library of original series and the convenience of watching content 'on the go' on Netflix; Kindle fire stick or Apple TV to stream content directly on your device. The key product values here are constantly updated content, convenience of watching and, in certain cases, like Amazon, affordable pricing. An annual Amazon Prime membership comes with free delivery, free video and free music for the price of four coffee runs. If you look at the Raymond man, he hasn't changed much. His look may be edgier, more modern, but the basic values are the same: traditional, patriarchal, conservative, protective of the family institution, generous but with a sense of noblesse oblige (think of the scene with the grown-up student in a vaguely Mayo College avatar gifting Raymond to his beloved retired teacher) and the future man of the house. A Raymond advertisement will rarely mention the cloth, yet, a large number of upper-middle-class Indian families will choose the fabric because of the values it is associated with.

3. Keep your message focused, using the power of threes and the power of one. Limit yourself to one or two key messages, and use the 'power of three' and 'power of one'. Too many messages runs the risk of cognitive overload which make your audience tune out. This is especially true in the post-Covid-19 era as the bulk of our communication is carried out via short videos or social media posts. A firm that does this very well is Zomato. Their July 2020 advertisement conveys: 'It is safe to order from Zomato.' In less than thirty seconds, the ad manages to relay the message using a conversation between a mother and her son on safe food delivery. The son explains how it is safe to order from Zomato by detailing the safety measures taken by the company, and the mother is convinced. One message, three sub-messages to convey the key point of food safety.
4. Put your personal charisma to work. It may be useful to look at political campaigns for cues on how political leaders use their persona to shape mass narratives. While the Prime Minister Narendra Modi is an obvious example of the product (Narendra Modi) and the brand ('Acche Din') seamlessly melding into a winning sale. Our political (communications) favourite is Lalu Prasad Yadav. Once Paarul had covered him as a young reporter at TV18 (now Network 18). At that time, he declared to an audience of international investors at Pragati Maidan, Delhi, 'I want computer chips, not

potato chips.' His message was on point; a simple and significant statement for a business-minded audience. Many Indian businessmen have perfected this art. Let's decode their personal styles and observe their compatibility with their business brands.

If we ask you the names of some of the top businessmen in India, you would probably say Ratan Tata, Mukesh Ambani and Anand Mahindra. All of them reflect a certain personal chemistry with their firms that helps convey their messages. Ratan Tata stands for a certain set of values and ethics that sync well with the Tata brand. This enables him to speak out (which he does carefully and not frequently). If you visit his Twitter page, you will find him commenting on issues as diverse as animal rights to calling out 'fake news' about him and the work of Tata Trusts.[3]

By contrast, Mukesh Ambani uses his persona to convey his business vision at a grand scale. He can't be goaded into a response till he is ready. Having once run into him in the 1990s at the Ministry of Industry and Commerce while reporting for ABNi Dow Jones, I (Paarul Chand) saw him drive up in an ordinary Maruti car with two other people riding with him. If one of the people with him hadn't tipped me off about his identity, I wouldn't have known who he was. At a time when TV cameras weren't as pervasive as they are today, he was totally calm in front of the mic and camera thrust in his face. He kept smiling and walked away without answering a single question about the purpose of his visit.

The new-age CEOs, especially the startup CEOs, are comfortable using their personal equity to convey their message. Xiaomi India's Managing Director, Manu Jain frequently poses with his products and pushes them strongly on social media channels. In 2019, when Xiaomi hired a new corporate communications head, the announcement was made tagging Jain and the Head of Marketing Anuj Sharma, in a rather fun tweet, which revealed that the technology journalist Ankit Vengurlekar would now be leading the PR and communications function at Xiaomi. One of the pictures showed Vengurlekar, a yoga enthusiast, showing off a headstand with Sharma and Jain standing alongside.[4]

Then of course, there are the highly storied Flipkart co-founders, Sachin Bansal and Binny Bansal. Sachin Bansal actively used Twitter to share his points of view. In fact, both of them even delivered goods to customers during their Big Billion Days campaign in 2015.[5]

You may have noticed that all of these examples are of male CEOs. Interestingly, there are very few examples of women CEOs in India using their persona for communicating. Bollywood entrepreneurs and film stars like Anushka Sharma and Deepika Padukone are among a few exceptions. About twenty-five years ago, Enron International's Rebecca Mark (before the notorious debacle at the power manufacturing firm), made a strong impact during her India visits. Articulate, confident and charismatic, her presence made a difference, leading to media-packed events.

We may see a change in this respect though as a new leadership emerges in the wake of Covid-19. We already have Tanya Dubash as executive director and chief brand officer of Godrej Industries, as well as Roshni Nadar Malhotra when she took over as the chairperson of HCL Technologies in July 2020, becoming India's first woman head of a listed IT firm.

It will be interesting to watch how they interact with the external world. So far Roshni Nadar Malhotra appears to be fairly reticent and low-key. On the other hand, Tanya Dubash has been very outgoing, impressing her personality at events, like L'Affaire, a food and hospitality platform curated by Godrej.

5. Preparation, preparation and preparation is the key. Unscripted messaging may work for improv theatre, but not for key business messages. To give you an idea: the visit of any major global CEO to India will be planned months in advance, with detailed briefing books written by their communications team. These would include redflag questions and appropriate responses, so that at no point will the CEO be unaware of what needs to be said. A CEO's statements become public almost instantaneously, therefore a lot of preparation is needed on key messaging points to sound effortless.

To understand the kind of preparation that must go into this, take a look at the celebrity special, stand-up comedy show *One Mic Stand*. It is hard not to be inspired by the amount of effort guests like Shashi Tharoor, Taapsee Pannu and YouTube star Bhuvan Bam put in.

Ashish Gupta, ex-CEO of telemedicine firm Docprime, clearly explains how a CEO would look at defining his messaging in collaboration with the corporate communications team. Ashish says, 'There is an operational and execution side, and there is a conceptual philosophy side to brand messaging. I [Ashish Gupta] for one find it very uncomfortable to see that somebody can actually take over the conceptual messaging of the brand. That has to be defined by the CEO. The corporate communication[s] team's role then would be an "outside in" approach and they would analyze the message and say, "This is what the customer wants, these are the channels where we can reach these types of customers; we can create PR campaigns around this." I want to keep my PR [message] very, very focused on crafting the actual messages around what our story is.'[6]

Explaining how the messaging is often arrived at, Ashish says, 'I believe that after the doctor, who heads our customer chat, and [me], it's my head of corporate communications that is the one person who has read and gone through the maximum number of customer chat[s]. Normally you wouldn't expect a PR professional to do that.'

This is because Ashish's corporate communications head would have gone through the customer chats, even suggested new features and functionalities to the product team. 'The reason you see my corporate communications head do that is because she has gone through so much data. Therefore, you have all those light bulbs going off, which is a rare thing. I haven't seen that depth of research going on before, and very often she will come back and give a product feature from the chats.'

According to Ashish, the nuanced messaging for their stakeholders has been impactful: 'One of the biggest values I have from PR [is] that I know that in healthcare, I can practically reach out to anyone and I won't have to say what Docprime is – everybody has heard of Docprime. We haven't [produced] a single advertisement. Nobody has seen an Akshay Kumar dancing for us.'

How do you define your own messaging as CEO? Here is a matrix that could help.

This is a sample communications message matrix drawn from the public statements of the home essentials and furniture brand Ikea in India:

Mapping Your Brand Message

Main Message	I stand for high quality with low costs, respect for the environment and a great place to work.	I care for the environment.	Fifty per cent of my employees will be women.	I will offer furniture for rent.
Proof	Company's code of ethics.	Use farm waste such as straw to make products so that they are not burned and air pollution is reduced.	Hiring policy and inclusion policy in place.	Rental website up and running.
Main Audience	Employees	Customers	Customers, especially women	Customers, especially millennials
	Suppliers	Media	Media	Media
	Customers	Government	Government	
Desired audience takeaway	I will buy from this company. I want to work for this company.	This is a responsible company. I will buy from this company.	This company believes in inclusion for their own and societal growth. I want to work for this company. I want to buy from this company.	I and my friends are part of the gig economy and this company understands us. I want to buy/rent from them. I want to work for them.

To sum up, a CEO may design his or her brand message keeping in mind the following tips:

- Know your brand story: the reason why your brand exists.
- Customers provide you with rich data and feedback about refining your message.
- Plan micro-messages that target employees, segmented customers, government and other influencers.
- Constantly check for consistency and the tone of messaging.
- Prepare a list of words that can and cannot be used in your content, especially when referring to sensitive issues. Do we say challenged or differently abled? Should we refer to caste or class distinctions? Is our note formal or informal? Look at the AP stylebook for examples and formulate your own messaging stylebook.
- Know your Overton window. The Overton window in communication refers to the range of issues the public will tolerate about a brand or a person. First devised to measure issues politicians can talk about to potential voters, it is just as useful for brands to know the range of messaging around the brand.

We conclude with one terrific example of how messaging from Narendra Modi's playbook has crystallized and changed over time. In 2014, Modi's message was 'Sabka Saath Sabka Vikas', presenting a united development platform. In 2019, before the elections, understanding that the elections were a referendum on his reputation, Modi took the challenge head on with the slogan 'Phir Ek Baar Modi Sarkar' (Modi for Prime Minister again). The principal messaging shifted from one of development to one of Indian identity built around the projection of Modi as a defender, protector, saviour and nationalist. This itself was split into two sub-messages: anti-Gandhi/Congress and pro-nationalism.

When he won a thumping majority in May 2019, the post-election message shifted to: only two castes in India, one that is poor, and the other that wants to help the poor. This, in itself, is a remarkable public shift in messaging coming from the Prime Minister directly. After that, he tried to limit the damage caused by statements of members of parliament such as Pragya Thakur, by asking his party and ministers to not speak in front of the cameras. At the same time, he also expressed his support for the minority. All these messages were designed to blunt national and international criticism of his right-wing approach and shift the narrative away from caste and religion to class.

The year 2024 will reveal the success of this new messaging approach as Modi will be required to play the Hindu card in the face of other challenges such as the economy, India's Covid-19 response and border tensions with China.

***

Mukesh Ambani offers yet another example of smart messaging. His handling of the sale of 32.9 per cent of Jio shares to major global players such as Google and Facebook, the global investment firm KKR and the private equity firm Vista is noteworthy.

This is how the flow of communication took place:

1. In 2019, Mukesh Ambani announced Reliance's intention to be a zero-net-debt company. In summer 2020, Ambani (with remarkably few media leaks) rolled out announcement after announcement of the sale of Jio stakes. Notably first in the series was the big-ticket announcement about the Facebook investment of over ₹ 43,000 crore.
2. In July 2020, during the Reliance Annual General Meeting (a major messaging event in itself), Mukesh Ambani delivered two key messages that had been saved for exactly such an occasion. One, that Reliance was now a zero-net-debt firm. Two, that Reliance would be developing its own 5G technology. He made the announcement with his back against a massive canvas which declared that the 5G decision was dedicated to the vision of Modi's 'Atmanirbhar Bharat'.
3. This was a meticulously executed messaging strategy: a carefully planned starting point (the announcement about Reliance becoming a zero-net-debt firm), specific messaging around reaching this goal (the sale of the stakes in Jio) and the big bang conclusion (developing their own 5G technology).

The 'smart CEO', post Covid-19 will be someone who puts effective, strategic and human communications at the centre of his regular outreach at work. At the end of the day, there is nothing more human than communicating and CEOs often do not get a chance to tap into their human side at work. This could be one way to do that.

5

CEO'S ROLE #3: DRIVE BRANDING

A CEO's Personal Brand

AT THE INTERSECTION OF marketing metrics, products and brand value is the CEO. The CEO brings their personal brand to the company and its brands.

According to Kalaari Capital's Vani Kola, 'The C in CEO could be communications. Communications is central to the role of the CEO. But I think in the cacophonic world we are in today, it's important to step back and think about this whole notion of communications. Communications is both verbal and non-verbal, and actions speak louder than words. It is important for CEOs to think about communications in a more holistic way. There are a lot of very successful CEOs who don't do a lot of public communication. Through history, there are quiet CEOs who have delivered phenomenal value. Communications is about providing clarity that creates alignment among various stakeholders. It's like a general in a war. Or a conductor in an orchestra. I read about a research that analyzed how conductors communicate with their orchestra. Some are flamboyant and move their hands around, others are quiet and communicate with just a look or a nod. Both are very effective. It's about the personal style. It's about finding alignment with your people.'

Sometimes CEOs, especially founder CEOs, become synonymous with the brand, for example, Bill Gates and Microsoft, Steve Jobs and Apple, Mark Zuckerberg and Facebook. Closer home, N. R. Narayana Murthy defined brand Infosys.

When Murthy and the first non-promoter managing director of the firm, Vishal Sikka, came to a disagreement about how the firm was being led under Sikka, it set off a chain reaction that eventually resulted in Sikka's exit. At the heart were several governance issues. These eventually translated into a difference in values as embodied and communicated by Narayana Murthy and Sikka.[1] While Narayana Murthy stood for thrift, economy, a technical-engineering-styled mindset and financial conservatism, Sikka came to embody the opposite. He travelled by private planes and came across as flamboyant compared to the economy-flying Murthy who carried his own luggage. These perceived and perhaps very real differences played out with Murthy publicly questioning corporate governance at Infosys under Sikka.

Many experts we spoke with agreed that this mingling of the CEO and a company's brands perhaps works in the early days of the company but as the company matures the CEO's personal brand needs to be distinct from the company's brand. The dangers of over-reliance on the CEO's brand are very obvious.

In 2018–19, Flipkart was redefining the brand's reliance on its star promoters Sachin Bansal and Binny Bansal. With Walmart values coming into the picture after the famed buyout, the parent firm acted swiftly when #MeToo allegations surfaced about Binny Bansal.[2] He resigned quickly even though the complaint was found to be uncorroborated after an independent investigation.

There are other brands that have had to deal with over-reliance on their CEO brand, such as star founders like Paytm's Vijay Shekhar, Tesla's Elon Musk, Uber's Travis Kalanick and AirAsia's Tony Fernandes.

One CEO who balances his personal and company's brands well is Anand Mahindra. He influences the brand without becoming the brand. He confines his communication to Twitter, and his tweets are as much about his personal experiences, passions and fears as they are about the Mahindra group's achievements.

When Jeff Bezos faced a scandal surrounding his divorce and his leaked naked selfies with his girlfriend Lauren Sanchez, he used his personal stature and declared war on the media. He published his version of the story about attempts by the *National Enquirer* to blackmail him over his revealing personal pictures and messages. As owner of the *Washington Post,* he could have pushed his messaging primarily through the paper, but he chose to publish his defence on the blogging platform *Medium*.[3] He may have done this for two possible reasons. It limited the broadcast of his personal story as he used a platform he could control. Secondly, it helped him keep the story away from his company, Amazon. If he had chosen a mass media outlet to tell the story, he would not have been able to control the narrative and distance the story from the company.

However, on 8 February 2019, the day this extraordinary blogpost was published, Amazon's stock dropped by 1.62 per cent, a massive drop in share value. Once again, this is proof of the intricate relationship between the CEO's and the company's brand.

Align Your Personal Brand

In the preceding paragraphs, we have outlined how CEOs interact with their brands. The takeaway from these examples is to align your personal brand as the CEO with that of the firm.

To return to Narayana Murthy, his personal values aligned very well with the Infosys brand values of being ethical, frugal and growth oriented.

Richard Branson, meanwhile, is well known for his pioneering and adventurous brand, which he reinforces by flying solo across the Atlantic in a hot-air balloon. This tied in well with the firm's aviation business. His frequent hot-air balloon adventures helped raise the profile of the Virgin Group dramatically. It also established the Virgin ethos as being 'delightfully surprising, red hot and straight up while maintaining an insatiable curiosity and creating smart disruption.'[4]

Seamlessly aligning yourself with your firm's brand values in words and action requires a high degree of consistency. The corporate communications team can help you keep track of this.

As CEO, how do you build your personal brand? Here are a few suggestions:

1. Choose your channels of communication. Do you prefer video or the written word? If it's the latter, use short videos on LinkedIn or YouTube. Post strategically; a CEO should not overexpose themselves in videos. And remember: quality over quantity. In fact, most Indian CEOs hardly ever opt for video, Twitter or even LinkedIn, unlike their international counterparts, like Mark Zuckerberg who uses Facebook Live frequently to talk to his stakeholders.
2. Zomato's Deepinder Goyal uses his Twitter handle very well to communicate regularly. A 10 July 2020 tweet (one of the several that day about their latest company results) announced financial rewards in the form of ESOPs for Zomato employees who took voluntary salary cuts after the Covid-19 breakout.[5]

   Goyal is also someone who has demonstrated strong empathy for his staff and society at large, especially during the coronavirus pandemic. Zomato's excellent Feeding India programme is a case in point. So is his refusal to service a client who wanted a delivery man of a certain religion only to deliver his food.[6] Goyal declared that they were not 'sorry' to lose out on business if it came in the way of their values, adding, 'We are proud of the idea of India – and the diversity of our esteemed customers and partners.'

3. With the Covid-19 crisis restricting space in mainstream media, the situation is ripe for CEOs to successfully use platforms such as LinkedIn and Twitter. And for the brave, video platforms such as Reels on Instagram and Live on YouTube and Facebook are available.
4. Are you quick on the draw, or do you prefer to think a lot before posting? If it's the former, use Twitter or write long-form blogs on LinkedIn, Medium or WordPress. Anand Mahindra, yet again, is a perfect example of well-thought-out Twitter posts. His account on Twitter should be a mandatory reading for CEOs hoping to build their personal and company brands.
5. Speaking at high-profile events is a great way to present your point of view, as is being a part of top-flight juries. Today there is a plethora of webinars and virtual events to choose from; but pick one that suits your profile, expertise and comfort level. Many CEOs will not speak unless the co-speakers are their peers or ministers or the audience is very large. The profiles of the speakers and overall visibility matters to CEOs when picking events for participation. Every time you have such an opportunity, prepare your messages and comments

in advance. Practise them with your communications team. Take a look at the Reliance Industries annual shareholder meeting videos to understand the level of preparation that goes into such events. Any of the CNBC and the *Economic Times* events are also good but heavily sought-after platforms.

6. Be prepared to be published in mainstream media. This means meeting reporters who may not always be friendly. Here is one example of how Grofers CEO and Co-founder Albinder Dhindsa handled a difficult reporter who was convinced that Grofers was broke. He actually showed the reporter the Grofers bank account details to prove that the firm was indeed solvent.[7]
7. Align your personal brand with that of the company. The CEO brand should be in sync with the firm's brand. In his businessman avatar, Karan Johar is perfectly in sync with his brand. Fashionably dressed, highly articulate, seen with his peers often, artsy but with Bollywood roots intact, the extension of 'Brand Karan Johar' with jury roles on reality shows and his own TV shows; the effort he puts into being seen and supporting his films is completely in sync with being a top-flight Bollywood director and mover and shaker of the cinema world.

In an ideal world, the CEO's brand image improves with the company's. Here is one way to think about the intersection of the company's messaging with the CEO's brand.[8]

RAISING THE CEO'S BRAND

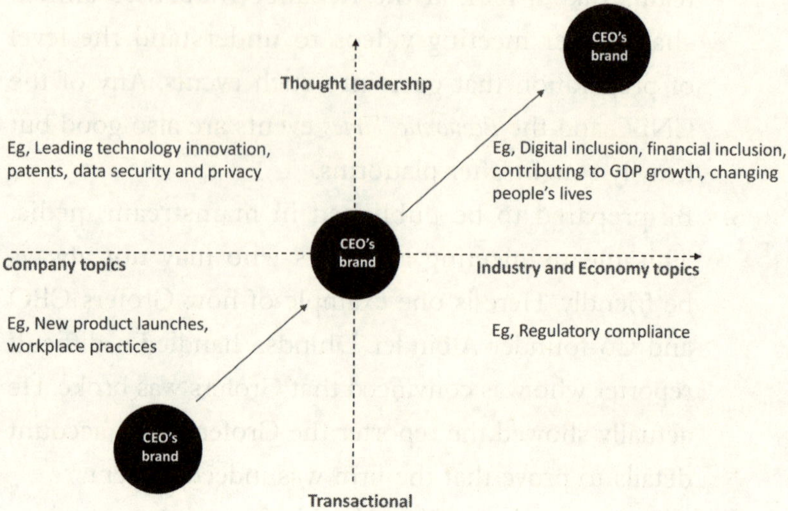

What does the above grid signify?

1. The CEO's brand is first established when they begin to engage with their external and internal stakeholders regarding product or service launches and comment on workplace or operational issues. These issues are mostly tactical and transactional but help announce the brand values of the CEO.
2. As the CEO becomes more comfortable with their personal brand, the brand can be extended to comment on other issues such as regulatory compliance and the policy environment.
3. The CEO's brand achieves fruition when the CEO starts commenting on what is known as 'thought leadership' issues that help establish the CEO as a

respected and credible authority on matters beyond the company's products and services.

4. At this stage, the CEO's brand has gone up significantly along with that of the company, as they now comment on larger issues to do with the country and different aspects of the civil society.

6

CEO'S ROLE #4: BE A GOOD SPOKESPERSON

THE YEAR 2018 WAS extraordinary for American CEOs. Perhaps never before in the history of corporate America has there been a larger number of top CEOs speaking in one voice against a government policy. Not just any government policy, but specifically Donald Trump's notorious family separation policy that separated children from their parents, family or other adults accompanying them at the US–Mexico border. And it was not just any CEO who took a stand against Trump, but the who's who of America's corporate world: Apple's Tim Cook, Chobani's Hamdi Ulukaya, Cisco's Chuck Robbins, Facebook's Mark Zuckerberg and the US Chamber of Commerce's Tom Donahue, among many others. Their resistance helped support a national protest against Trump's policy, which was eventually withdrawn in June that year, just two months after it was announced.

This is CEO-communication at its best. The support of

America's CEOs was critical to making the issue of family separation mainstream. Undoubtedly, involvement in political rows is an extreme measure, but there is scope for better use of communications for their corporations. A CEO's empathy or lack of it, especially in Covid-19 times, can cause their brand to move up and down the stock market. We believe CEOs who cannot communicate their empathy and inclusivity are at a distinct disadvantage in today's world.

Let's look at another example. Based in the US, Business Roundtable is a coalition of the top CEOs in the country committed to the growth of the US economy. In the wake of the Covid-19 pandemic, Business Roundtable was quick to issue a statement saying, 'Extraordinary work has been and continues to be done by large US companies to safely support the economy and deliver essential services to American families across the country through this unprecedented economic disruption. As the nation undertakes the work of economic reopening and recovery, Business Roundtable CEOs will continue to work with policymakers at all levels and experts to enable a safe and rapid recovery.'[1]

The Busines Roundtable website also lists specific initiatives taken out during the pandemic to support the effort to fight it.

It's interesting that there hasn't been any such CEO roundtable initiative in India that can provide a platform for CEOs to express their views on larger issues, though there are of course industry coalitions such as the Confederation of Indian Industry (CII) and the Federation of Indian Chamber of Commerce and Industry (FICCI). While many have shared individual responses to Covid-19, but there has been no concerted and united statement by Indian CEOs on their collective approach to the pandemic. Of course many Indian firms are working behind the scenes to support the government by providing PPE kits, hospital space in hotels and feeding families, but specific organized joint commentary on how the businesses are being hit in this situation from the CEOs is missing from the communications narrative.

How have CEOs handled this pressure to communicate earlier? The big difference pre and post-Covid-19 is that CEOs could ignore some of the issues outside their immediate sphere of business. However, the seismic shift that Covid-19 has caused means that society and business are evolving and to be seen and heard matters more than ever now.

Pre-Covid-19 Issues for CEOs

In order to understand the current circumstances, it would be helpful to look at the kind of communication challenges faced by CEOs in the pre-Covid-19 era.

It's afternoon on 6 September 2018, and the Supreme Court of India has just read down Article 377, thus decriminalizing homosexuality in the country. Meanwhile, there is news of mob lynching by cow vigilantes in a city where you have 200 of your employees. At the same time, the news of the arrest of alleged Maoist activists and a possible Bhim Sena demonstration in the city where your headquarters is based comes in. #MeToo campaigners have named more alleged offenders and one of them is, maybe, a senior leader in your organization. Meanwhile, the Reserve Bank of India has announced its latest slack season credit policy; there may be a new e-retail policy announcement that may mean reconciling some verticals in your firm. How do you respond to all this? Do you *need* to respond to all this?

No, you don't. But in the unprecedented Covid-19 times, there are some key issues which CEOs must be ready to speak about; they need to preferably build an ongoing external (aimed at the government, customers, media and society) and internal communication (aimed at employees):

1. **Employee Welfare**

   Regarded as a soft subject before Covid-19, now it has become imperative to speak out on the safety, stability and future of a company's employees. CEOs are well aware of this. An April 2020 survey by the *Economic Times* revealed that thirty-two per cent of the CEO respondents considered employee welfare to be their top concern.[2] Almost forty per cent of the leaders pinpointed that frequently communicating with employees during these uncertain times to be the most important measure they have taken to curb negativity arising from this crisis.

   As per the report, 'Stay home, stay safe ... stay strong ... we are there for you. Support all the junior employees and support staff of the key associates' was Saugata Gupta's message to his peers. Saugata is Managing Director and CEO of Marico, one of the largest Indian FMCG companies.

2. **Future of the Firm, Sector and Economy**
   Tech Mahindra's Managing Director and CEO, C. P. Gurnani has been doing well in this sphere. In a recent article in *Quartz India*,[3] he spelt out his top tips for dealing with the business changes for a company brought on by Covid-19. He said to corporate leaders, 'Be a wartime general to overcome this crisis – business leaders will have to fundamentally change from being peace-time leaders to wartime generals. During a war, generals do not have the luxury of time, and so they need to think fast and act faster. The current situation calls for leaders to be focused and yet open to revisiting strategies, to take bold risks, to judiciously deploy their resources, and above all, to work tirelessly till the war is won.'

   In the same article for *Quartz India*, he also adds a good lesson for Indian CEOs which is that they need to be seen and heard more during the pandemic. 'We have to accept that the post-pandemic world will not be the same as before. What will help us win this war is our ability to seize this new normal and define it for ourselves. It is pertinent to ask: Are we the leaders who our teams can trust to take them home safely? Do we command that level of faith in our teams? I hope the answer to these questions is a resounding "yes".'

3. **Showing Authentic Empathy**
   In the current scenario, showing authentic empathy and being vulnerable in public will go a long way for CEOs; being truly communicative with stakeholders

> is now essential. Satya Nadella, for example, sent a personal email to Microsoft employees in March 2020 just as the Covid-19 pandemic was exploding.[4] While outlining the work that Microsoft was doing at the time across sectors, including taking certain financial measures for Microsoft partners, Nadella also spoke about his pandemic-induced concerns and anxieties. This was a complete communication. He commented on Microsoft's Covid-19 response in detail, spoke about specific partner measures and shared his own anxieties about his wife's ageing parents in India.

In addition to the qualities mentioned above, for a CEO to be a strong spokesperson, here are a few recommendations that we received from several CEOs we had interviewed for this book.

Recommendations for Planning CEO Communication

Choose a Topic that Resonates with You

It is definitely not necessary to have a personal or organizational position on everything, but you do need to pick an issue you have a genuine interest in and that connects well with your brand's emotional profile. Emotion (and not technical product or services) drives better connections with audiences. For example, for the Mahindra group, nation-building through social entrepreneurship (as evidenced by their social entrepreneurship platform 'Mahindra Rise for Good') and inclusion are important emotional and ethical brand values.

This is further reinforced by certain tweets posted by Anand Mahindra, and him lending a helping hand for the education of young Aseesh Parihar[5], whose father cycled over 100 kilometres to get him to the exam centre, or admiring the dedication to fitness by badminton champion PV Sindhu.

Develop a Position

After you have chosen the topics that matter to you and your organization the most, develop a position. Let us map, for example, how the data privacy issue played out. It has been said that data is the new oil. On the face of it, it has been an issue that has affected only social media organizations such as Facebook and WhatsApp that collect large amounts of data. But every firm collects data in some way or the other. In pre-Covid-19 times, at corporate office buildings around the world, we saw a casual collection of visitor data, much of which was personally identifiable. Where is the data stored? Can we demand that our data be deleted after the visit? Data is collected at all points today. But what is a company's data protection policy? When developing a position on data privacy, organizations have to think about how, when and from where they collect data even if it is something as harmless as the visitor entry register at their offices. What fresh challenge does working from home pose on data security? With board meetings happening online, confidential company data is even more at risk.

It is, therefore, important for firms to not only have a data security policy that takes into account work-from-home but also ensure that the policy is publicly available to consumers in an accessible manner; not just the small print version, which frankly nobody reads.

Communicate Strongly

Does the topic need to be communicated internally or externally, or in both ways? That would depend on the topic or issue and the stage of progression the issue is at. Your choice of words and platforms can create credibility for your brand or erode your brand.

Recently, it was revealed that FreshMenu, an Indian food startup, failed to reveal a data breach impacting 1,00,000 users in 2016. This prompts us to think about 'first responder crisis communications'. When news about such an issue breaks, the responder is usually the seniormost executive in the organization – the CEO or founder. In the case of FreshMenu, Founder CEO Rashmi Daga put out a statement on their website.[6] Parts of it are reproduced here:

'You may have seen Twitter posts and media articles about a data breach at FreshMenu back in 2016. I owe every user of FreshMenu a sincere apology for the breach and for not addressing this matter proactively ... The stolen information comprised of names, email-ids and phone numbers. At no point during this time was information such as user passwords or payment related information, breached.'

The statement goes on to share information on how the data is being stored and audits taken for checking the system security. The statement ended with a brand message of what FreshMenu stands for (of fresh food cooked in a nearby kitchen) and provided ways to contact the CEO.

Here are a few suggestions that could have made this statement better:

1. '... audit our system' is too general and vague. What is the timeline of the audit? What will be done with the information from the audit? Will new measures be announced? A new data collection policy? After audit results are out, will the organization plan wide communication of remedial actions? It might have helped to provide a stronger solutions response.
2. Stating that only names, phone numbers and emails were leaked is not reassuring to the customer who fears misuse of their private data. In the hierarchy of data leaks, financial and medical data is the most sensitive. But leaked names, emails and phone numbers also pose risks.
3. The full statement also included the following: 'Anand Prakash, India's best-known white hat hacker ...' But 'best-known' is a subjective statement in this case. Crisis response must always be factual and precise.

Let's look at another example. On Jack Dorsey's visit to India in 2018, he held up a poster that read 'Smash Brahminical Patriarchy'.[7] The photograph unleashed a firestorm helped along by the high-profile journalists who attended the meeting where the poster was held up. Without saying a word, Dorsey made it to the headlines in India. While this may be in keeping with Dorsey's persona of making political statements (his tweets on Myanmar being a case in point), it proved to be a PR nightmare for Twitter in India. (Not that you saw people abandoning Twitter.)

For communicators, the question is: Would he have been better off by not raising the issue at all? The communications team is bound to have alerted him about the consequences of such an act. But if he was looking to highlight the issue anyway, it worked superbly. The danger lies in the fact that given the complexity of the issue, a poster can be a very reductive tool for raising one's voice.

Brahminical patriarchy is an issue few Indian CEOs would dare to address openly. But in an age of CEO and employee activism where consumers look to business leaders to fill a certain moral vacuum left by the political class, it may work very well.

Research bears this out. People trust their employer and expect the CEO to advocate for change, says the 2019 Edelman Trust Barometer.[8] It is true for Indians too. Out of the 1,150 respondents surveyed in India eighty-four per cent trusted their employers to do what is right, mirroring a global trend in rising trust in employers.

The study also found that seventy-nine per cent of Indians surveyed expected the CEO to lead the change rather than wait for the government to do so.

2019 EDELMAN TRUST BAROMETER REPORT

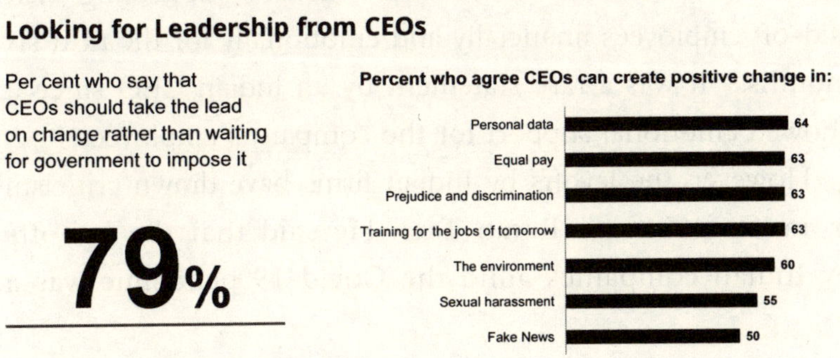

While this survey was done pre-Covid-19, many CEOs post-Covid-19 have been fairly vocal about their support for their employees, not simply leaving it to the government to provide job protection measures. Rishad Premji, addressing his first annual general meeting as chairman of IT major Wipro in July 2020, told the investor audience that not a single Wipro employee had been laid off during the Covid-19 pandemic. Furthermore, over ninety-five per cent of Wipro's global workforce had been enabled to work from home. Making this statement at the AGM affirmed Premji's take on the issue in front of a formal audience and during the company's most important annual meeting.

CEOs such as Make My Trip's Deep Kalra, Bajaj Auto's Rajiv Bajaj, Ola's Bhavesh Agarwal, OYO's Ritesh Aggarwal and Paytm's Vijay Shekhar Sharma, all announced a hundred per cent pay cut for themselves to show solidarity with their employees.

When layoffs became unavoidable for firms such as Zomato and Swiggy, both firms also had the CEO announce the news (in May 2020) and came up with support measures for the laid-off employees.[9] Zomato's CEO and founder Deepinder Goyal even tweeted that Zomato would be supporting their laid-off employees financially and emotionally for the next six months.[10] It was a rare statement by an Indian CEO since it showed emotional support for the company's employees.

However, the layoffs by Indian firms have drawn criticism from Tata Group's Ratan Tata. He said that the lay-offs by Indian companies amid the Covid-19 pandemic was a knee-jerk reaction and show a lack of empathy among the top leadership. 'These are the people that have worked for you. These are the people who have served you all their careers. You send them out to live in the rain. Is that your definition of ethics when you treat your labour force that way?' he said in an interview with YourStory.[11]

Practice

D. Shivakumar says that a CEO must undergo three rounds of media training before meeting the media for the first time. As an experienced corporate executive who was the primary spokesperson for large brands, he should know. Training and practice are not only necessary for communicating with the media, but also large groups of employees, partners and customers.

Marketeers talk about last-mile engagement, but the lack of a proper spokesperson can result in the failure of any attempt at such an engagement. Of course, there are people like Donald Trump who defy this logic, but that is a black swan event and very tough to pull off. Investing in spokesperson training, therefore, is one of the best investments a CEO can make. It is critical to their success and the success of the brand's reputation.

How to be a Great Company Spokesperson

1. Invest in training.
2. Don't write out your quotes in full, write down the keywords. This will allow you to be spontaneous.

3. Designate a devil's advocate from your communications team who can throw some tough media questions at you. Don't fire that poor person later!
4. Dress and talk the part.
5. Practice like you have to run a marathon. Practice is key to being a good spokesperson.
6. Practice the art of the fifteen-second sound byte. If you need to break it down: five lines of copy makes for a fifteen-second sound byte.
7. No harm in saying you don't know something. Don't hesitate to say, 'I will get back to you.' But make sure you do get back.
8. Study the speeches of good speakers. Narendra Modi is arguably the best orator in India today. His slogan 'National Ambition, Regional Ambition' was a clever play on the word NARA. Dhirubhai Ambani was an exceptional speaker with his ability to connect with his audience. Anand Mahindra, Nikesh Arora, Ratan Tata and R. C. Bhargava are some other notable speakers from India. Internationally, Steve Jobs stood out as a compelling speaker.

7

CEO'S ROLE #5: BE INCLUSIVE

MOST GLOBAL BRANDS SELL or operate in over 100 countries. Many brands claim to be present in 200 countries in the world.[1,2] As organizations with global growth aspirations enter new markets around the world and hire people from outside their home country, cultural differences in the workplace have become a reality.

In the mid-2000s, while working for a multinational in India, one of the authors hosted a team of Asia Pacific communicators for their annual team meeting. One female participant from another country complained to the host that a certain meeting coordinator, who was a man from India, was insensitive to her need for personal space. Apparently, this meeting coordinator stood too close to her while interacting with her. Those of us who live in crowded spaces, may sometimes have a blunted sense of personal space. The example cited is a clear case of cultural insensitivity. As the world gets smaller with high-speed travel and Internet-based communications platforms, workers, especially white-collar ones, are forced to interact with people different from themselves. The difference may be social, economic, gender, sexual orientation or abilities-based. These differences get amplified during meetings, project management and social outings, and show up in the form of conscious or unconscious bias. These biases hamper the cultivation of a sense of 'belonging' and affects morale and ultimately productivity.[3]

A BetterUp research published in the *Harvard Business Review* revealed, 'If workers feel like they belong, companies reap substantial bottom-line benefits. High belonging was linked to a whopping 56 per cent increase in job performance, a 50 per cent drop in turnover risk, and a 75 per cent reduction in sick days. For a 10,000-person company, this would result in annual savings of more than USD 52 million.'[4]

Why should CEOs Care?

There are several established studies that demonstrate the correlation of a diverse workforce on positive top-line and bottom-line growth in business. In one such study, McKinsey in 2018 estimated that $ 28 trillion can be added to the global economy if women fully participate in economic activities. That was about a thirty-five per cent increase in the global economy.

Nirmala Menon started her diversity and inclusion (D&I) focused consultancy, Interweave, nearly two decades ago. In 2019, she responded to a few of our questions on the subject. Reiterating the need for diversity, she said, 'Any progress that has happened in this world has happened because someone thought differently from the rest. So, diversity of thinking under the watch of an inclusive leader is what creates the innovative products and services that we enjoy.'[5]

There are many examples of new products and market expansion when companies recognized and catered to minority customer groups. In 2013, Microsoft launched a smaller controller for their Xbox product for women who have smaller hands as compared to their male counterparts. The new game controller also catered to adolescent gamers.[6] Later in 2018, Microsoft also launched an adaptive controller for gamers with limited mobility abilities. According to a Nielsen survey, reported widely in India in 2018, between the years 2009 and 2016, the men's face cream market doubled in size and that of face wash grew sixty times. Men were definitely not a primary audience for the manufacturers a few years ago.

Micro-inequities and Micro-aggressions

With the evolution of science, we have gained better knowledge about minority groups and people with abilities that may be different from widely visible and acknowledged human abilities. Menon says, 'It is established that there are 150 kinds of biases that can play out in interpersonal interactions – either at work or in life.'

Differences can also play out as micro-inequities[7] or micro-aggressions[8] in the workplace. For example, in the middle of a meeting the boss's behaviour may be different when different people are presenting their ideas. It can be a subtle change in demeanour unnoticed by anyone else in the room. The presenter might wonder: 'What I did to invite such a reaction? Is my boss even interested in my idea?' It can lead to a sense of insecurity and a feeling of unbelonging.

In the Covid-19-induced work-from-home world, interactions between colleagues has moved online. With technology still lagging in providing us with life-like meeting experience, we have to depend on verbal communication to signal inclusion. This may be done by the deliberate use of inclusive words and tones of voice. The introverts, the soft-speaking and the mild-natured have always found it difficult to speak up in meetings. Creating a safe environment in the online meeting space for the minority groups to be included and heard is a leader's challenge and opportunity. Menon adds, 'Recognizing the bias and proactively working to overcome [it] will make us more productive at work and help us lead fuller lives.' As understanding of prevalent differences among people increases, organizations are looking for more ways to be more inclusive and sustain a sense of belonging among both their internal and external stakeholders.

Dr Billy Vaughan of Diversity Training University International, California, categorizes organizational inclusion cultures into five different kinds. These may also be stages through which one organization may progress in its own inclusion journey.

1. At the **Conventional** stage, there is resistance against any discussion on diversity. Some people in the organization believe they are superior to other groups. There is an aversion to cultural differences and very

low awareness of cultural diversity. But attitudes may change when such people have to adhere to government regulations or industry compliance requirements.

2. At the **Defensive** stage, inclusion initiatives are accepted under pressures (of regulation or compliance needs), but people in such organizations consider inequality to be a natural result of differences in different groups' abilities.
3. The **Ambivalent** stage is the stage at which equality is valued but there is low cultural competence to check bias. Personal bias is overlooked and organizational bias is highlighted which ought to be checked. Therefore, people may experience non-inclusion at a personal level, but things may seem to work well at an organizational level. About 12–15 per cent of people recognize the importance of diversity in such organizations; their diversity and inclusion journey has begun.
4. At the **Egalitarian** stage, both organizational bias and personal bias are curbed and most employees experience what the organization claims as its diversity and inclusion framework. But stereotypes still exist, and is room for improving the cultural competence of employees. The leader of such an organization recognizes that diversity makes the organization more competitive. They also recognize that the brand gets more recognition in the market due to its inclusion policy.
5. At the **Inclusive** stage, the organization and its people experience harmony between cultural beliefs, values

and behaviours, and employees have a very high degree of cultural competence. Everyone has the opportunity to rise to the top of the organizational pyramid.

The CEO can move an organization from stage 1 to stage 5 with the help of their D&I, human resources and communications experts. According to Dr Vaughan, leaders can make everyone understand the connection between the role of diversity, inclusion and business impact. CEOs must champion diversity and inclusion for the organization to progress to the next logical stage.

Rooting out Bias is a Leader's Responsibility

In *Hit Refresh*[9], Satya Nadella writes about a widely denounced answer he gave to a question at one of the US's largest IT industry women's conference – the Grace Hopper Conference of 2014.[10] When asked what advice he would give to women who are not comfortable asking for a pay raise, he had replied that doing good work is like good karma and rewards usually follow in the future, if not immediately. That evening he wrote a long email to Microsoft employees and apologized for answering the question 'wrongly'. By then most of the global media and social media had reported and questioned the validity of the response. Microsoft's women employees in India hated Nadella's response, a rare emotion displayed by employees for an otherwise much-loved CEO.[11] Nadella had clearly answered the question from the point of view of his personal journey and how he had navigated his career. As he answered that question, he was not thinking of people who may have been victims of conscious or unconscious bias and exclusion.

Reminiscing the Grace Hooper event in his book, Nadella wrote, 'Leaders need to act and shape the culture to root out biases and create an environment where everyone can effectively advocate for themselves.'

Fostering an environment of high-level inclusion takes work. Good people practices, transparent and unambiguous policies, and empathetic leaders are important. Communications can bring them all together. Vicky Bindra, Chief Product Officer at FIS, says, 'There are two people who I feel I need to partner with very strongly to drive diversity and inclusion. One is the HR head and the other is the communications head. If you partner with these two really well, honestly, you can conquer the world. That is because these are the people who are touching the pulse of the organization every day.'

Nirmala Menon shared with us in an interview, 'Communications is critical in building an inclusive culture. It is the only way to get meaningful engagement from diverse quarters of an organization. Clear and honest communication will allow for safe and candid conversations, which then allow for innovative ways to deal with the situation. In fact, open and honest communication is more than half the battle won.'

In September 2018, Anand Mahindra, Chairman of the Mahindra Group responded publicly to an incident in which a former employee had accused his manager of homophobia.[12] This reaction was also the most prominent corporate India response to India's Article 377. The response was fast, sharp and unambiguous, helping reassure anyone who had doubts about the Mahindra group's position on the subject. He wrote 'I can categorically assure you that we celebrate diversity in our workplace. Our Code of Conduct is explicit on this subject. Fairness and dignity of the individual is enshrined in our core values.'[13]

Using Communications to Drive Inclusion

1. Honestly assess the climate of inclusion in the organization based on feedback from employees, partners and customers. These could be in the form of all-employee surveys, special inclusion assessment surveys, equal pay and pay gap analysis. Or it may be a way to quantify intangible feedback about trust and belongingness.
2. Set up proactive communication channels to reach out to diverse groups of internal and external audiences and communicate the commitment to inclusion in town halls, blog posts or all-employee emails. Communicators can help CEOs share their inclusive messages with personal commitment and authenticity. For example, Satya Nadella was not proud of his answer at the Grace Hooper Conference but he accepted his mistake and used the incident to drive an important message within Microsoft. He wrote to employees, spoke about the speech in town halls and discussed it in his book. His commitment to inclusion was believable.

3. A global organization with diverse groups of employees must develop neutral language and behaviour guidelines that are respectful and empathetic to different groups of employees, suppliers or partners. Communications and diversity experts can work together to define the guidelines of an organization. I (Gayatri Rath) worked with an American colleague who, during long meetings, would put his feet up on the tabletop. He did it quite naturally without realizing how offensive it was to the Indians in the conference room. In another example, American workers especially those in the technology industry, start emails by addressing a person by his/her first name and without a 'Dear ...' or similar salutation. Many people in South Asia feel offended by what they think is an abrupt and rude start to an email. In a third example, when referring to blind people, some organizations use the phrase 'visually impaired'. But is that the right way to describe a blind person? There is a strong point of view emerging among D&I experts according to which it is patronizing to use euphemisms such as 'differently abled' or 'visually impaired'.
4. Convey the organization's commitment to inclusion to the external ecosystem such as partners and industry peers. For example, supporting minority community suppliers, like women-run businesses, to succeed. Or by participating in industry and media discussions on the topic to clearly articulate the organization's commitment which will both influence industry peers and assure employees.

5. Prepare a communications policy and standard ways to refer to communities and people with challenges.

Menon summarizes these points very well: 'Diversity is a fact of nature and exists whether it is visible or invisible ... Being more accepting and less judgemental of each other and looking at differences with curiosity and as an opportunity to learn from rather than a problem to be solved is a good way to start with the varied aspects of diversity and their intersectionalities.'[14]

In organizations with global ambitions, the CEO is expected to be the chief diversity mentor if not the chief diversity officer. A strong people plan and a strong communication plan can help CEOs build a stage 5, highly inclusive organization, where employees have a clear sense of belonging.

8

THE COVID-19 CEO AND THE EVOLUTION OF COMMUNICATIONS

I (PAARUL CHAND) CAN clearly remember what I was doing when the Covid-19 pandemic marked its entry in India. I was working on a sponsored '30 under 30' list for the public relations sector, after having just returned from Mumbai from the jury meet for deciding this list.

People often talk about what they were doing when the news of the world's most impactful and calamitous events hit them. The assassination of President John F. Kennedy or former Prime Minister Rajiv Gandhi, or when the airplanes hit the Twin Towers on 9/11.

The pandemic is today's catastrophic, life-altering global calamity. And all the science and technology and economic power in the globe cannot immunize us from its long-term impact.

There are two groups of professionals who are bearing the brunt of leadership at this turning point, these are, politicians and CEOs.

Therefore, there has never been greater focus on CEOs and how they are speaking, acting and behaving, that is to say, communicating during Covid-19. CEOs have to allocate a far greater portion of their time communicating with their stakeholders than ever before.

Here are some deep-seated changes that have occurred for CEOs in the wake of the pandemic:

Working Remotely and Online is Mainstream

Online communication is now mainstream. One could not have made such a claim even at the beginning of the year 2020. Now, with restrictions on offline movement slated to continue for the unforeseeable future, CEOs have begun to rely on online and digital means of communications exponentially. Some of these channels include online video calls, webinars, online panel discussions and virtual town halls.

However, an August 2020 study by the US-based National Bureau of Economic Research shows that work-from-home and online tools not only cause fatigue but have also led to the average workday lengthening by 48.5 minutes, and there has been a 12.9 per cent increase in the number of meetings per person per day.[1]

The white paper also provided the first large-scale analysis of how digital communication patterns have changed in the early stages of the pandemic. It observed that there was a rise in the number of people marked on every email as well as the attendance at internal meetings.

But the biggest change for a CEO is that centralized office-based communication has reduced dramatically, forcing CEOs to be more radial and less top-down in their communication strategies with employees. They also have to work harder to stay engaged and motivate their colleagues during online interactions.

Breakout Communication during Covid-19

As the saying goes, the situation often makes the leader. According to Vani Kola, 'Any crisis requires rethinking, special thinking and communications.' She says a crisis requires companies to be authentic, open and empathetic.

An excellent example of good crisis communication is how New York Governor Andrew Cuomo has communicated since the Covid-19 breakout. New York was the early epicentre of the pandemic in the US, peaking with over 9,000 daily new cases in mid-April 2020.[2] Between March and October 2020, Andrew Cuomo impressively stuck to a relentless and effective communication schedule which included daily briefings, staying on message, relying on data and repeating the instructions for safety.

According to Professor Ian C. Woodward, a specialist in leadership and communications and the Director of the Advanced Management Programme at INSEAD, 'During every press conference, Cuomo utilizes the rule of three to support his message: "Stay Home. Stop the Spread. Save Lives." This follows the sequence: "action, problem and empathy". His dialogue is authoritative, demonstrating command of issues and facts; his actions and voice show deep personal commitment and resilience.'[3]

Woodward also explained that both Cuomo and New Zealand Prime Minister Jacinda Arden were zealous about:

1. Overcommunicating in short bursts so that there were frequent but short updates. This ensured that the latest and most credible official information is regularly available.
2. Sticking to the three ideas in one message rule. Arden and Cuomo both stuck to calls to action that were clear and succinct and contained no more than three ideas; as is clear in Cuomo's message. Arden combined her message to stay at home with regular video casts from her own home to emphasize the point.

Ethics and Compassion are a Key to CEO Communication

One major change that Covid-19 has wrought is that being compassionate and ethical has never been more key to a CEO's communication strategy. Jane Nelson, Founding Director of the Corporate Responsibility Initiative at the Kennedy School of Government, Harvard University, said in a recent article, 'The first and foremost thing [CEOs] can do is lead through demonstration. When I talk about corporate leaders, I'm referring not just to chief executive officers, but site managers, or regional managers in companies. They should also show they care – because this crisis is fundamentally about people's lives. Leading with empathy and a sense of connection with employees, business and community partners and customers is key, as is acknowledging that no one has all the answers.'[4] Nelson added that CEOs are also responsible today for policy communications with governments around the world.

(See Annexure 4 for response by Business Fights Poverty, a live beta mapping tool of company actions being funded by aid from the UK government. The database lists examples of actions being taken by companies to identify and scale up innovative solutions, through their core business capabilities and operations, philanthropy and social investments, and their engagement in policy dialogue and help towards strengthening institutions.)

Phase 1 of Pandemic Brand Communication: People not Brands First

The first phase has highlighted a big change brought on by the pandemic. This has to do with CEOs now having to find a way to project their brands, products and services via the lens of people and communities. This is quite an incredible shift in communication. It is a shift that has been coming ever since the advent of social media as individual voices began to matter more than ever before. While this shift was underway, Covid-19 acted as a super catalyst – the fuel that burns through for a rocket launch – heightening the need to connect and communicate with people first when talking about brands.

Every brand worth its salt has tried to do so. Uber, Zomato, Mahindra and Mahindra, Tata, Reliance, pharma firms, Godrej, ITC and Nestlé have all demonstrated their human side since the outbreak of Covid-19. Their CEOs have consistently brought up the larger society and economy angle. CEOs like Rajiv Bajaj have tried to take the view that the lockdown has not helped[5] only to find their comments quickly politicized and attacked. Professor Ian C. Woodward commented that Daimler CEO Ola Källenius did the right thing by clarifying in an interview with BBC, 'We have two priorities: first and foremost, the health and safety of our employees around the world.' Woodward explains that it was only later that he mentioned the second priority: 'the health of the company'. He progressively explained actions being taken to help employees and manage cash and supplies. He gave examples of Daimler staff donating masks from car paint shops to healthcare workers.

This is borne out by Edelman's 'Special Report: Brand Trust and the Coronavirus Pandemic', that came out in April 2020. It shows that Indian customers want brands to do the right thing during the Covid-19 crisis. And that they will base their future buying decisions on how brands demonstrate their concern for employees and society at large. Consumers want CEOs to take the lead in this situation.

EDELMAN'S 'SPECIAL REPORT: BRAND TRUST AND THE CORONAVIRUS PANDEMIC'

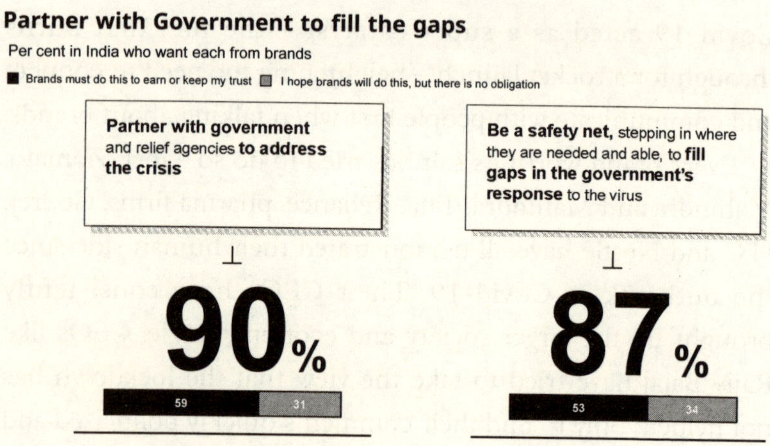

Additionally, one of the ways brands can gain their trust is by partnering with government and relief agencies to address the crisis, with fifty-nine per cent of Indian respondents saying that brands must do this to earn or keep their trust.

The first five months after Covid-19 was declared a pandemic, from March to August 2020, set this communication approach firmly. July–August onwards, this has begun to shift again, bringing in some much-needed nuance into how brands and CEOs are communicating now.

Phase 2 of Pandemic Brand Communication: Evolving to Product and Services and Economy

In this second phase of people first, as people get on with earning a living, CEOs will be able to touch upon the following communication pegs in greater detail while linking the brand with the realities of Covid-19. This phase has already begun and is full steam ahead.

1. Brand communication that acknowledges the reality of using a product or service during Covid-19. A recent campaign by United Colours of Benneton saw their India CEO Sundeep Chugh talk about celebrating kindness warriors who had been at the forefront of helping people during the pandemic. Interestingly, the word Covid-19 is not prominently mentioned in the campaign; the hashtag is #UnitedByCause. The cause being making an impact by helping others.[6]
2. Motivating people while working from home or at office with social distancing.

3. Specific solutions for operational and pipeline challenges. It will be more constructive if CEOs focused on solutions rather than simply highlighting the problems.
4. 'Atmanirbhar Bharat', 'Make in India', have become a major communication peg for CEOs during Covid-19, but this needs to be negotiated carefully as many companies are dependent on international procurement systems across sectors.
5. Productivity techniques that are personally tried and tested by CEOs is of great interest to the public.
6. Future growth and survival of their sector and brand.

III

USING CORPORATE COMMUNICATIONS

9

BUILDING TRUST CIRCLES

THE SUCCESS OF A brand is connected to trust and perception, according to Suresh Narayanan, Managing Director of Nestlé India. He would know. Speaking with us in late 2018, he told us about the Maggi ban crisis his company had weathered. At the time of a national ban, Maggi, one of Nestlé's flagship brands in India, commanded a whopping eighty per cent of the market share in its category. To comply with the ban, Nestlé India had recalled and destroyed nearly 38,000 tonnes of the product.[1] The recalled product was incinerated in industrial kilns. Narayanan jokes that houses built in India during those months perhaps have a little bit of Maggi in them! Nestlé successfully fought the ban with the help of reports from independent laboratory tests. About six months later, when the brand relaunched, it took less than three months for it to regain its market leader position in its category.

Narayanan attributes the power of a brand to three circles that surround it. The first circle is the core. As a consumer, what is our personal experience with the brand? That forms the core of the brand and the value it delivers. The second is the circle of associations. What does the consumer associate with the brand? In the case of Maggi, is it healthy? Is it hygienically produced? The third circle is the public face of the brand or as Narayanan describes it – the cause. Does the brand mean more to the consumer than its immediate functional value? In the case of Maggi, does it mean more than just a tasty snack? Does it impact society in a larger way? Does Maggi generate jobs? Does it help farmers prosper? Is it committed to reducing the carbon footprint created during its manufacturing process?

As consumers of brands, we interact with a brand and ask these questions every day. The sum of these experiences makes us love the brand or not.

Trust is Tested in Moments of Truth

Vicky Bindra says, in the context of fintech brands, 'In our business, trust is the only thing that can help us grow ... there are some critical points of failure or "moments of truth" that actually engender trust or take away trust ... the first is, problem resolution. That is very high on the list of people thinking of trust. Are you solving my problem? Two, do you stay with me in my time of need? And three, are you supporting and bringing options to me that I couldn't think of?' Bindra says brand trust is a result of how the brands respond to the customers' needs during the moments of truth.

The moment of truth may not be just a point in time, that is, when a customer walks into a shop to buy a product. These moments may span days, months or years depending on the industry and type of product or service. For instance, the Covid-19 crisis has spanned several months and continues to impact governments and businesses around the world. Government agencies are being tested every day. Their response to the evolving situation has been a test of the trust of the citizens.

When a twenty-year-old broke into a CRPF cordon and launched a suicide attack killing over forty paramilitary personnel, how did the government of India respond? Did they resort to jingoism with an eye on the upcoming elections or did they speak as a responsible country that seeks a permanent seat at the United Nations Security Council?

In another example the 'moment' spanned a few hours on Twitter when Larsen & Toubro launched a hostile bid for controlling stake in IT firm Mindtree in early 2019. The Mindtree team responded on social media alleging corporate bullying. In response, the L&T leadership spoke of 'compassion' and 'empathy' in their communication. The Twitter episode tested the maturity of both leadership teams in what was a moment of truth for both parties.

Each interaction with the brand creates more trust or depletes trust. In their 2018 report titled 'Bottom Line on Trust', Accenture defines trust as a consistent experience of competence, integrity, honesty, transparency, commitment, purpose and familiarity.[2] Their research showed a clear correlation between trust and the company's bottom line.

Using a Moment of Truth Well

According to Bindra, one cannot 'wing' communication during these moments of truth. Communication needs to be well thought out and nuanced. The communications team can help CEOs and leadership teams by better mapping and assessing moments that are important in the life of a company. The team can also help build a culture where every employee, partner or distributor feels empowered to take the right decision in a moment of truth. Above all, the communications team can help with the nuanced articulation of messages that are inclusive of all audiences.

A Common Purpose and Shared Understanding

A vision, mission and a clear set of values are the safeguards for any organization when the moments of truth present themselves. An organization that has been able to align its employees, partners and distributors around a common purpose is able to use each moment of truth to grow its brand. Narayanan attributes the strong Nestlé values as the power that helped them tide over the crises arising out of the Maggi ban.

Singapore Foreign Minister Vivan Balakrishan said in an interview to CNBC in March 2020 that the country's social capital of trust and compliance among citizens was a contributing factor in containing Covid-19 in the early months. This social capital of trust and compliance was built over decades.

Suppose you run a consumer product company and customer delight is one of your core company values. A customer is feeling cheated and has called your call centre to demand a refund. Your company policies do not allow your service centre executive to give a refund under that specific case. In fact, a refund will mean lower incentive for the service centre executive. What does your service centre executive tell the customer in such a circumstance?

1. Does he/she argue with the customer?
2. Do they assure the customer of the company's best intent and explain why they cannot refund the amount?
3. Do they try to convince the organization that the customer's point of view is valid, and even though it means lower service incentive, it would be correct to refund the amount?

How the service centre executive responds depends on how well he/she has imbibed your company's value of delighting customers.

Focusing on the Most Important Audience

Any organization may have ten to twelve different audience groups that they regularly interact with or need to influence to get their work done. These may be core audiences such as employees and customers or other audiences such as media professionals and analysts.

The Accenture report 'Bottom Line in Trust' lists customers, employees, suppliers, the media, analysts and investors as the key audiences with whom to build trust. In the case of financial services and fintech industries, the regulator may be a very important audience. It is important for an organization to identify three or four key audiences that are most important to them. The company's anchor communications programmes are then decided based on how the company would like to interact with these audiences.

Recognizing the Moment of Truth

Trust-building opportunities may be different in different socio-economic situations. The Edelman Trust Barometer, an annual research conducted by global communications consultancy Edelman, found that for many years commercial organizations and their CEOs had become more trustworthy than governments. This changed with the Covid-19 outbreak. Trust in governments grew tremendously through the pandemic.

The food delivery company Zomato was faced with a moment of truth when a customer refused to accept a food order because it was allegedly handled by someone who belonged to a religion different from his own. Zomato used the moment to articulate their inclusive values and as a significant media moment. They recognized the opportunity and used it to their advantage.

Anand Mahindra's response to a former Tech Mahindra employee's allegation against a homophobic manager helped cement trust in the Mahindra brand. At the same time, Facebook's lack of a fast and clear response to Cambridge Analytica's misuse of its data eroded trust.

Articulating the Message Well

The actual words used to communicate during a moment of truth can make a difference between overreaction or underreaction to a situation. It can augment or erode trust in the brand.

During a crisis or a developing situation, a good sentiment analysis and assessment can help in deciding the tone of communication. Does the situation demand an empathetic tone or an assured, controlled tone? An unempathetic CEO can worsen a crisis situation. A widely talked about example is the British Petroleum CEO's comment on TV: 'I'd like my life back ...,' after a disastrous oil spill in 2010 off the coast of Florida.[3]

In summary, trust is built during moments of truth. An organization that is geared well to recognize and use such moments of truth, can build trust faster than those that are not. The CEO, their leadership team and communications experts must work together to build organizational trust circles.

10

MANAGING CRISIS

Managing Crisis in the Age of Instacomplaint

IN THE EARLY 1970S was born the angry young man of Bollywood, played by the inimitable Amitabh Bachchan. With a blue shirt carelessly knotted at his waist as a shipping dock worker, or donning the khaki uniform of the quintessential Bollywood police officer or swapping identities with the Don, Bachchan (or Vijay the iconic character in the Hindi movie *Deewar*) took on the system swiftly felling corruption, injustice and the system itself.

Nearly fifty years later, social media has given rise to another 'angry young man'. It is the customer, who is not necessarily young or a man. The customer is often up for an instacomplaint (or an instant complaint) against a product, service, employee or company. The customer's first port of call is no longer a brand's customer care (never too trusted in India and other parts of South Asia, in any case) but Twitter or Facebook. The gap between last mile delivery of a brand's values and the customer has now found a platform that connects with an audience of tens of thousands or more.

This is one of the biggest crises any brand handles today. Running like a constant low-grade fever, it can suddenly flare up and burn the brand in seconds. Add to this the Covid-19 development where the C-suite is expected to be far closer to the customer than ever before, the active rise of digitization has made customer engagement a permanent area of crisis communication management. Covid-19 itself is of course a meta-crisis situation for any company, that will dictate how companies communicate in the time to come.

Before social media changed our world, media houses decided how to position a negative story, which could be controlled and confined to certain media channels. Today, due to the development of 24X7 TV news that began in the 2000s, the rise of the Internet and the ability of any customer with a phone to turn into a broadcaster and the sheer scale of that broadcast has changed matters completely.

In 1994, while covering the Andhra Pradesh state elections (for BITV, the now shuttered TV arm of *Business India* magazine) I (Paarul Chand) managed to get a late-night TV interview[1] with the late P. V. Ranga Rao, the son of then Prime Minister P. V. Narasimha Rao who was seeking re-election as the MLA from Hanamkonda in Warrangal. He gave me a rather indiscreet interview criticizing his father obliquely. When the interview was published, few people noticed the criticism. Today, one cannot think of the son of a political leader criticizing his father (that too, if he was the Prime Minister of India) and not cause a major incident on social media![2]

In April 2017, a spat broke out between a passenger of IndiGo airlines and the ground staff. While subsequent reports showed that the passenger instigated the row by physically grabbing ground staff, a video of the incident went viral and Twitter was flooded with irate customers sharing their own unpleasant experiences with the airline's service staff.[3] To add to the airline's woes, a month later, badminton Olympian PV Sindhu tweeted about rude ground staff who did not allow her to board an aircraft with her sporting kit.

Together these incidents sparked a great deal of debate about the airline's service. These two 'presenting incidents', as they are called in psychological terms, triggered a period of backlash against brand IndiGo.

In 2019, brand IndiGo was on the verge of another crisis, this time related to developments in the aviation industry in India. Interestingly, the 'presenting incident' in this case was the closure of Jet Airways, a rival airline. It had created two sets of perceptions about the brand. First, it had gained a lot of praise for uptaking some of the gap in service after Jet shut down. Second, the reported differences between the founders in the wake of the narrative about how the promoters of Jet Airways crashed the airline led to negative investor sentiment. IndiGo, which commanded nearly half of the market share, saw a fall in its share price by nine per cent in May 2019, after the news of the row between the promoters.[4]

What should IndiGo have done? While the firm's CEO wrote to employees reassuring them of management stability and its growth strategy, we did not see a public engagement with the customers through media or social media stories, offline events or otherwise. The brand needed a more comprehensive crisis communication strategy.

Mapping Crisis Communication

Airline's Stakeholders	Suggested Communication Action
Financial Institutions	Direct engagement, banking focused publications
Customers	Stories in mainstream media, travel publications, online loyalty programmes, segmented customer engagement, social media
Regulator and Government	Aviation seminars, social media, mainstream media, public affairs programme

Let's look at another ongoing brand crisis, this time to do with Huawei. The Chinese firm, as a result of being blacklisted by the US government as a threat to national security, has seen companies such as Google and Microsoft withdraw operating systems Android and Windows from Huawei products.

Huawei continued to deny links to the Chinese government and defended its brand. Its communications in pre–Covid-19 times managed to counter the controversy (in spite of its US PR firm Edelman breaking ties). Here are the highlights of Huawei's communication outreach:

1. They made quick announcements about alternate operating systems.

2. Effective linking of the firm with Chinese nationalist sentiments. News reports say that Apple phone sales have actually declined in China, and Huawei sales have gone up. Pro-Huawei statements are being made on platforms such as Weibo.
3. The overwhelming sentiment among the US media is anti-Huawei. The *Wall Street Journal* published a detailed article on Huawei's alleged misdeeds, writing that 'Huawei's years-long rise is littered with accusations of theft and dubious ethics.'[5] Yet, ironically enough, the free press in the US also ensures that there is enough support for Huawei through the prism of trade barriers to technology, linking of security with trade barriers and former President Trump's overall derogatory and inconsistent communication.

Was this enough for Huawei? It doesn't seem so as national security has taken over the conversation. Apart from Covid-19, the conflict with China in Ladakh has now made India's initial decision to allow 5G technology from Huawei uncertain. In September 2020, newspapers reported that Indian telecom firms such as Jio and Airtel have filed additional applications listing firms such as Samsung and Nokia as their preferred 5G equipment partners.[6] Jio has even said that it will use its own technology for 5G trials.

The banning of fifty-seven apps in India post the Galwan Valley border conflict in June 2020, including the very popular TikTok India and PubG shows how much 2020 has changed the communication environment for corporates. Countries such as the US are also exploring a ban on TikTok.[7]

Since the ban, according to news stories, TikTok has taken several steps to indicate their independence and separation from China including hiring international, non-Chinese CEOs and engaging with their influencers on TikTok.[8] Their CEO had been front and centre with communication, addressing among other things how responsible TikTok is and why it is essential for TikTok to exist to offer healthy social media competition. He also took potshots at Instagram's Reels feature that is very similar to TikTok.

TikTok CEO Kevin Mayer, in July 2020, wrote an open letter saying, 'We believe it is essential to show users, advertisers, creators, and regulators that we are responsible and committed members of the American community that follows US laws.' Mayer is a former Walt Disney senior executive who left the firm in 2020 to join TikTok.[9] However, by August, Mayer had quit, his initial views overtaken by events that included a strong attack by former US President Donald Trump tried to force a deal that would see US ownership of TikTok via partnerships with Oracle and Walmart.

Finally, when the environment became extremely unfriendly to the business, the only way TikTok could change the narrative and communication was by distancing itself from its Chinese parent ByteDance. But even appointing a US CEO did not help stop the waive off hostility and lack of trust in TikTok's intentions.

Crisis: A Journalist's Point of View

As a reporter, the author's (Paarul Chand) aim was to find a story and report it. It wasn't really important whether the story was positive for a person or brand. It had to be viable, accurate and credible news though. A negative incident may feel like a crisis to a CEO or for a brand, but it is 'news' for the media. Brands and CEOs can sometimes get caught up in their own point of view and, therefore, inadequately represent themselves or their brands while dealing with the media.

Here are a few pitfalls to watch out for, when working with the media in a crisis situation.

As a journalist reporting in 1994 for India's first daily business show 'Business A.M.', produced by BITV on the national TV channel Doordarshan, I (Paarul Chand) covered a story on the proposed investment of a Japanese firm in an air-conditioning manufacturer in India. After filing the story, I received a very polite call from the promoter of the firm asking me to remove any mention about the proposed investment as it had not been formally announced yet. Full of the arrogance of a young, inexperienced reporter with a national audience, I declined abruptly. The promoter very politely accepted my decision. If I tried to do such a story today, there will be SEBI (regulator) norms to consider, if the firm is a listed one. I am sharing this story to point out how internal dynamics work within a news firm. Many non-news organizations do not fully appreciate the ferocity with which a journalist clings to their story, especially after it has been published.

Secondly, for CEOs and spokespersons, it is easy to forget what one is saying and why, and disclose something inadvertently. As a television journalist, I was taught rapport building and told to make the interviewee forget about the camera and get them fully involved in the interview. Some of the interview guidelines were as follows: sit four to five feet from the subject; never show them the television monitor or their interview frame and ask them to look at the interviewer and not the camera. That put the interviewee at ease and helped them speak freely.

Thirdly, one error that CEOs often make, especially during a crisis, is thinking that their point of view matters to a journalist, and journalists will wait to run a story until they get the CEO's quote. A journalist hates to wait with a confirmed story and the CEO's point of view matters only if the story is advanced formally. If the reporter has a story that they have found out from other reliable sources, they will run it. They do not care if the CEO has commented on the subject or not. CEOs sometimes shut down communication with a journalist or delegate it to someone junior thinking that the story will go away or somehow get watered down as they themselves are not commenting on it. That does not happen.

Sometimes CEOs facing a crisis may think that a few positive stories in mainline media would solve the issue. It does not. CEOs need to pick and choose their communication channels, which could range from a WhatsApp group, a podcast or Facebook and yes, formal mainline media interviews as well. And one has to keep at it: listening, planning, acting, assessing impact.

To sum up, here are a few suggestions and takeaways for CEOs during a crisis:

1. Prevention is the best cure. Have a crisis plan and policy in place that maps the issues that could erupt in your business. Prepare a plan that can address

key stakeholders such as the government, customers, industry influencers as well as people impacted by your business. In 2017 and 2018, as Uber rapidly grew across global markets, it failed to proactively engage with policy makers and taxi unions in local markets and that resulted in two crisis-laden years prior to the company's IPO.

2. Set up a crisis communication centre to assess everything from employee and external communication, safety issues and operations. There will be high pressure on CEOs to communicate often. Resist the pressure to rush out and communicate, but make the communication with your audience regular, scheduled and predictable.
3. Your crisis team should include the CEO, the CFO, the legal head and the CCO (chief communications officer). In a crisis, the communications professional is the only person who has a 360-degree view of the business's stakeholders.
4. Use active listening tools (such as Cision, YouGov, Meltwater) to train your crisis management team.
5. Appoint a spokesperson and train them well. Don't hesitate to watch a few episodes of *Designated Survivor* on Netflix with Kal Penn as the White House press secretary or C. J. Cregg on *West Wing* (also on Netflix) to see how a good spokesperson carries themselves.
6. Data is your biggest ally in crisis communication. You will constantly need data to focus on your truth, to

segment audience and customize and communicate your messages to the audiences.

7. Among the new media customer, micro-influencers are the most important. Talk to them, engage with them.
8. Be clear about the news value of your message. News is the best way to push your angle. A good example is how well Narendra Modi travelled the story from development to nationalism during the 2019 elections.
9. Crisis communication is a marathon. Not enough is said about this but keep an eye on your stress levels during a crisis. Self-care matters. Have a counsellor at hand.
10. As Sun Tzu said in *Art of War*, in a war (and make no mistake that a crisis is war) always keep the high ground behind you.

Follow the above and chances are that you can bend it like Beckham during a crisis and turn it to your advantage.

11

MEASURING IMPACT

MEASURING IMPACT IS IMPORTANT for resource allocation in any organization. How should CEOs measure the impact of communications and align branding and communications budgets? We have worked with business leaders who assign communications budgets based on positive media stories promised for the year. Other business leaders have funded interesting new ideas to drive a business metric for the year. For example, when an IT product company was in the race to win the cloud top-of-mind recall, budgets were allocated to teams that worked to increase the online discussion and audience engagement on keywords such as 'commercial cloud' or 'artificial intelligence'. Inside several companies, measurement metrics may be aligned towards acquiring new customers. In a non-profit organization, it may be about enrolling donors. Sometimes it is focused on reaching a new group of influencers. Sometimes business leaders ask the question: how much sales will you drive with communications?

Does communications drive sales? We asked Bhaskar Pramanik what he thought of business leaders expecting communications to drive sales, and in response, he said that communications should be viewed through a broader lens as a strategic imperative for high performance and growth. But, at the same time, communications should have a clear mission, statement of purpose and measurable objectives that are aligned with the business' goals.

This is corroborated by communications industry veteran Dave Samson who told us in an interview that he believes communications professionals should be business people first. They must measure their success in terms of business metrics and not solely communications metrics.

For decades communications professionals have experimented with metrics that could capture the true impact of their work. Many professionals relied on brand perception studies while others have counted positive media stories and assigned a value to each story using a complicated formula. Share of voice, share of influence, advertising value equivalent, 'return on ideas' and 'return on objectives' have been used to measure the impact of communications.

A *Bloomberg* study published in the *Economist* put the average value of 'goodwill' in all listed companies in the world at thirty per cent.[1] For a company, goodwill is intangible in the shareholders' report. For an intangible value, thirty per cent is a high number. However, when you dig deeper, goodwill is backed by many tangibles, for example, a company's customer base, customer satisfaction score, number of products introduced or patents filed. Above all, it is the trust and confidence in the organization and brand. We think goodwill creation is a full-time job for communications professionals. Measuring goodwill is the best way to measure the impact of communications in an organization.

Stories Matter

Today we are operating in a very different world as compared to the pre-Internet world in which many of us began our careers. According to Dave Samson, in the new world demographics matter less. Shared interests, beliefs and experiences matter more. Stories are the vehicle for shared interests, beliefs and experiences in a community. They bind a community or a group of people – whether it is inside a company, housing society, city, religious sect or on a website.

The authors recommend that CEOs and communications professionals measure stories. How many good stories do you tell every day or every week? Do your stories generate positive conversations among your peers or online followers? Do your stories move people? Do they bring your reader closer to you? Sentiment measurement tools use big data and can help you answer these questions about your stories.

Influencers Rule but Influence has been Democratized

Before the Internet, brand influencers were movie stars, editors of newspapers or leaders of think tanks. In the Internet era, social media influencers have formed a new group that communications people and CEOs have to consider in their communications plan. These may be twenty-year-olds who, empowered by unlimited digital platforms and a fearlessness displayed by the millennials and Gen Z, can 'Instagram' what they want about your brand and get millions of people to propagate their view. Digital journalism newbies or YouTube stars can change the narrative about your new product in ways that were not possible before the rise of social media. Influence has been democratized. The ubiquity of access to broadcast platforms such as Facebook, Twitter and TikTok, combined by a newfound confidence to speak freely and publicly, has ensured that influence is no more the bastion of the select few. Any measurement metrics must therefore account for tracking and measuring the impact of these new influencers as much as they do for traditional ones.

Choose a Measurement Metric that Works for Your Brand

Devising a measurement metric requires clarity about the objective and impact. Why are we undertaking a particular communications outreach, and what do we hope to achieve by it?

Ray Day, former Chief Communications Officer at IBM, said at an event called Chai Talk, in 2019, 'If you can't measure it, you can't manage it.'[2] Ray believes that the meshing of storytelling with data insight is what matters as communications shifts from mass to micro-storytelling. To make the best use of data for storytelling, IBM now runs a content hub. One half of this hub is made up of data and analytics experts and the rest includes writers and video producers.

A little introspection and good planning can help you devise a set of measurable metrics that work for your business. Clear goals keep a communications programme focused. At the same time, it is important to guard against populist short-term activities. For example, a company can drive a large number of media stories based on exaggerated future plans. But the impact of these stories, should the said plans fall short, will hurt the brand in the long run. In another instance, if an organization is aiming to transform its sales process, media stories may not help. Stories about the success of the new process and sales role models in internal company forums – Yammer, Slack or Facebook – may help.

Also consider this. When launching the next big product, most consumer technology companies think of big, flashy launch events with movies stars and hundreds of news reporters. They hope to generate social media conversations and word-of-mouth buzz among traders and move the product in the market as fast as possible. Many product companies from other industries blindly follow this product launch template. But if your product is targeted at people who are not native Internet users and value the personal touch of your salespeople, a flash-bang launch approach and induced Twitter 'trending' may just be a waste of company resources. More importantly, it may be a distraction for your teams who could otherwise spend their time in more impactful activities.

Each organization needs to develop its own measure metric for its communications programme. What will work for a conglomerate like Godrej may not work for the Tata Group, and similarly what works for Walmart may not work for Future Group.

Samson points out that the impact of a communications programme is best felt, endorsed and conveyed widely by the allies of the corporate communications department in an organization. These may be the sales team, the product development team or the HR team. When the allies see impact, they push for larger communications programmes. We could not agree more. Communications never functions in isolation and operates as part of a broader network of teams.

Here are a few examples of metrics and frameworks organizations have used to measure the impact of communications. You may choose a combination of metrics that works for your organization or brand.

1. Perception and brand audits, trust reports and/or feedback reports using online or offline tools among important audience groups such as customers, employees, media, partners.
2. Social media sentiment analysis or a mechanism to capture anecdotal feedback from industry peers, for example: 'I saw your point of view on LinkedIn and I think you are right.'
3. Customer surveys and analysis of customer comments.
4. Anonymous comments on third-party online communities.

Here is a sample flowchart with hypothetical business goals to help a brand measure the impact of their communications initiatives.

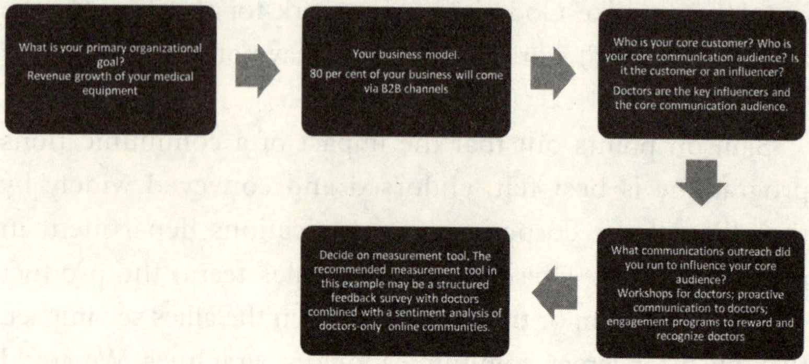

In our experience, the communications department usually finds itself in a tougher struggle for headcount and budget, than most other established departments. A relatively young and evolving function, it is yet to be fully understood by budget decision makers. A strong measure metric that aligns closely with business objectives and goals can change that. Creating an emotional connection with the audience and building trust will always remain core to building great organizations and brands. Telling evocative stories will never go out of fashion. Knowing how to measure the impact of these stories is the new fashion trend to embrace.

12

USING THE RIGHT TOOLS

IS THE MEDIUM NOW truly the message? The idea of 'public communication' is a bit of a conundrum, even more so in the post-Covid-19 social media age.

The Ashoka edicts are one of the early examples of press releases. A rock-cut statement directly from the top spokesperson, King Ashoka. Who would have read these massive pillars, some weighing as much as fifty tonnes? Let's say, people who lived in India, Nepal, Pakistan or Afghanistan – the areas where the edicts were discovered. Could you say all the people who lived from 268 to 232 BC read these messages? Probably not. You would probably have to live pretty close to the edict, know Prakrit or a bit of Greek and Aramaic, to read them. Very likely you would have to be a man who had access to education.

This is the heart of the oxymoron that is public communication. When communication is considered public, mass audiences come to mind. But naturally, the audiences are both mass and niche. A mass statement does not guarantee that the mass will see it. And this becomes even more complicated when social media is added to the mix.

Hyperlocal Living, Global Thinking Audiences

Today audiences are both hyperlocal and global. Your fresh-brewed coffee aficionado could be in your neighbourhood or across the Indian Ocean. Your voting public could be very specific to the city of Gurgaon or be more hyperlocal in the DLF colonies within Gurgaon. They could care about clean air, safe schools and organic food chains and pesticides, and equally they could care about caste and class discrimination. The latter are typically national issues, but your audience, which is hyperlocal, could care about national and global issues at the same time.

This boils down to a singular question of importance for any CEO. Who is your key audience or your key stakeholders? What is the impact of your communications strategy?

Speaking to us about the impact of communications, Ashish Gupta, former CEO of Docprime, emphasizes that it is about relationships: 'It's about how people who should be looking at me are doing so. Are they talking good about me, joining me as an employee ... partnering with me ... or even just having coffee with me and exchanging ideas?'

All communication has to be aimed, much as Joey from *Friends* aimed his furniture at the TV set, at these primary audiences. These could be:

1. People who use your products or services: your customers.

2. People who impact your sector: the policymakers, competitors, activists who may work on issues impacting your sector or influential investors in your firm who act as activists to force change.
3. People who may be affected or disrupted because of your product or service. For example, taxi drivers disrupted by Uber or offline retailers by e-commerce companies such as Amazon and Flipkart.
4. People you want to add to your customer base.
5. The mass media, print and television, that reaches your audiences.
6. Online versions of mainstream publications or video streams of TV stations which carry your message to your audiences.
7. Influencers, who strongly influence your customers and partners.
8. And of course, the almighty social media universe!

Smart Targeting and Measuring

At the beginning of this chapter, we asked a basic question: Is the medium the message? The answer is definitely 'Yes'. Oftentimes, the fastest and most effective way to reach your audience is through the mass media. In that sense, mass media still maintains its high relevance for CEOs and the brands they run. Getting your personal and company brand recognized by established newspapers and television channels is still a mark of credibility that outweighs visibility in digital and social media. This is true even in the post-Covid-19 world.

Newspapers and television clearly define the message they send out. In established print publications, the written word is backed by research and fact checks. In established television news, it's visuals (seeing is believing!). Human beings respond to mass media by relying on their evolutionary responses to words and pictures.

There are also many data-based tools that can really help target the right audience. Tools such as Prowly help you track the entire messaging journey from message pitch to media coverage. As a result, companies have the ability to target mass and niche audiences. Analytics firms such as Germin8 use artificial intelligence to align the CEO's message with the brand message. Boom Live!, a fake news monitoring site, can be useful in busting fake news about a brand. Cloudsek offers brand scan monitors that allow brands to monitor fake news and identify rogue apps and websites that are misrepresenting the brand. With data-driven tools, you can be hyperlocal in your targeting. YouGov offers polling to research issues at your fingertips. Meltwater and Talkwalker help you scan how your messaging is being received across social media channels. With the challenge of fake news entering the corporate sector from the political sector, tools to monitor, measure and alert brands about how their messaging is working are extremely important today.

What about Social Media?

Here's where it gets interesting. The impact of printed coverage amplifies when carried on the digital versions of newspapers. TV news is also available as a plug-and-play option. NDTV, for example, is available as a live stream on Kindle Fire. Republic TV is available on Hotstar.

But it's not necessary that mass media should lead the communication. Frequently, it's the other way around. If your focus is on a very specific audience that mostly 'hangs out' online, then that's where you should aim your communication. If your aim as a pharma company is to speak to moms and paediatricians, as Pediasure does, there is a good chance you may want to position your online communications at 'mom-prenuers' – moms who are entrepreneurs operating out of their homes. If you are an online mental health service platform, then logic dictates that your communications would need to be social media-led. If you are a brand that depends on offline bricks-and-mortar sales channels, chances are, your communication will form a mix of both mass and social media.

The key to deciding your channels of communication is audience relevance. Moreover, moving from likes and dislikes to audience engagement is important. You don't have to be super trendy, just relevant. If everyone is on Snapchat and you are an insurance firm, it may not make sense for you to be there. Snapchat may be influential, but may not be relevant for you or your brand.

How do you decide this, then? First, let's take a look at some of the tools of communication available to you.

Press Release

Press. Release. The two words conjure images of weighty import whizzing their way to reporters who are just one step away from Atticus Finch (the larger-than-life lawyer in *To Kill a Mockingbird)*. Nothing says public relations and communications at work more clearly than the press release, the penultimate communications tool.

Of late there is a tendency to dismiss the formal press communique in an era of statements via Twitter and Facebook. But before we critique and dismiss the humble press release, what CEOs and communicators must remember is that it is a formal statement from the company, with legal implications. Once a press release is issued on the company's letterhead, it becomes a legally valid document.

If you wish to share information informally, then do it as a background paper without the firm's logo, or as a verbal brief. The Ministry of External Affairs in India does this very well in their daily evening briefing. After the main statement is made and any written press release is distributed, it's pens down and cameras off! What follows is known as a deep-background, off-the-record oral briefing which is where sometimes the real narrative is revealed.

Other communications tools through which a CEO and their brand can find expression include:

1. Edit page or op-ed articles in newspapers
2. Press/Media conferences
3. Familiarization tours
4. Influencer collaboration
5. Media interviews
6. Speaking engagements at relevant and visible industry events

7. Television and other media panel discussions
8. Podcasts for masses
9. Webcasts for internal or external audiences
10. Guests on radio shows and talk shows
11. Messages on mobile messaging platforms such as WhatsApp and Telegram
12. Blogposts on digital platforms and social channels
13. Podcasts for specific audiences
14. Instagram Reels
15. Online events: panel discussions and webinars

Deciding on Your Tool Mix

Ultimately CEOs need to look at the PESO – paid, earned, shared and owned – model, while deciding on their communications tool kit.[1] With shrinking newsrooms in the post-Covid-19 world, earned media opportunities have dropped. It has given rise to paid and owned models of communication. This is where brands can better control their narrative through owned online platforms and properties. The use of subject or sector specialists, or influencers, is another communications tool that will see a sharp rise as customer audiences, now largely at home, expect greater authenticity and credibility from brand messages and messengers.

The grids below can be used to map your owned media and influencer strategy. The more questions you can answer in the grid, the more granular and impactful your use of communications tools will be.

Purpose	Audience	Strategy	Format	Voices Mix	Measure
Sector	Influencer opportunities	PR opportunities	Types of influencer activity	Audience	Measure
B2C	Segmented and targeted customer	Inform, make it official	Posts / Stories	Employees	Reach (monthly unique visitors) and engagement
B2B	Mobile customer	Format of story requires regular media	Instagram reels	Customers	Sample / Contest mentions
Food, Travel and Hospitality	Experience of product/ service matters	Government/regulatory impact need	Facebook groups	Competitions	Impressions / Shares
Auto	Trust ambassadors are needed / CSR	Leadership stories	Twitter	Business partners	Increase in followers / Likes
Tech	Micro audiences matter	Corporate results	Chat apps	Offline and online	Revenue

INFLUENCER TRACKING GRID

Purpose	Audience	Strategy	Format	Voices Mix	Measure
Sector	Government regulator	Social media channels/must have ethics guidelines	Social media	Owned media	Engagement rate
Brand loyalty	Customer	Own website	TV shows	Influencer mix	Reach (monthly unique visotors)
Reputation and values	Media	Offline channels	Podcasts	Celebrity influencer	Sample / Contest mentions
Marketing and sales	Segmented customer	Exclusive contents	Micro site	Media	Impressions
Inform	Employee	Map competition owned media	Newsletter	Business partners	Share of voice
Entertain	Mass or micro	Frequency	Chat apps	Customers	Event attendance ratio

OWNED MEDIA GRID

While often the medium is the message, the message does need multiple media channels to reach the intended audience, as the two grids above demonstrate. CEOs and their brands can learn from Ashoka. He used the written word when it was uncommon to do so, 2,200 years ago. He also used verbal communications modes extensively – sending messengers and emissaries all over his kingdom and to foreign courts, to propagate his beliefs and messages.

In the modern world, CEOs have several platforms to build their brands. A few of these are:

1. **Voices:** CEOs have access to powerful voices. The CEO's voice itself is very powerful for the brand. They can also rely on other voices in the organization and in the ecosystem, such as happy customers and partners.

2. **Allies:** Third-party influencers such as industry analysts or industry think tanks or sector specialists can be allies who help propagate the company's or the brand's message. Of course, that relationship has to be value- and trust-based. A brand cannot buy such a relationship.

3. **Moments:** Key moments are a great opportunity to put out key messages. Many industries have a tradition of annual awards and annual conferences. Many companies also observe such traditions. Oracle OpenWorld is an annual event, and every year in the fall the city of San Francisco turns red, the Oracle brand colour. Fifty thousand partners, customers

and employees gather to learn about the newest developments in the organization.

4. **Imagery:** Imagery conveys the company's or the brand's identity and personality. Imagery can be the posters on your notice boards, on presentation slides, on exhibition kiosks or in your advertising. And in today's world, a branded virtual backdrop.

5. **Stories:** Finally, perhaps the most important platform available to companies and brands today are the stories they can tell. Stories of struggles that were conquered, diseases that were overcome, lives that were changed or how environment was protected.

Aligning voices, stories, imagery, allies and moments will give brands, organizations and CEOs a unique tool with which to communicate with all categories of audiences.

Many Indian CEOs have done a good job of keeping trust in the brand alive. Zomato CEO Deepinder Goyal, Anand Mahindra, Ratan Tata, C. P. Gurnani of Tech Mahindra, Rajiv Bajaj have all been very actively communicating during Covid-19 times. But have they fully explored the communication tools available to them? We think, not yet. The potential lies limitless in the post-Covid-19 world to create more open, transparent and effective communication between a CEO and their extended brand family.

13

THE FIVE ELEMENTS OF COMMUNICATIONS

THE FIVE ELEMENTS OF communications are like the five elements of nature in ancient Indian belief: water, air, fire, earth and space. Just like the five elements of nature sustain life, the five elements of communications – voice, images, moments, allies and stories – give life to good communications. They help your audience connect with you, your brand and your message.

Choose the Right Voice to Convey Your Message

Like most children, Gayatri's son hated eating vegetables and loved pizza for lunch. Jamie Oliver's pizzeria was his favourite eating-out place for years, to his parents' chagrin. Oliver was his hero. One day, on a food show on TV he heard Oliver recommend eating five fruits and vegetables every day. That did it! It made the teenager conscious of what he eats every day, and how much healthy food he needs to compensate for the junk he eats. As a mother, Gayatri cannot thank Oliver enough for it!

The right person or personality – we call it the 'voice' – can deliver a message more effectively than a thousand screaming advertisements. The voice can impact business growth and behaviour change. The 'voice' is usually someone with credibility either because of their position or their expertise. Religious leaders are usually powerful voices, as are CEOs of companies. The voice may also be a character that has established its credibility over time such as Ronald McDonald or the Amul girl.

To communicate a brand's or an organization's position well, choosing the right voice is important. If you want to portray yourself as a technology-driven company, you may use your chief technology officer more often. Or prepare the CEO to speak about technology innovation with as much conviction.

Images Convey more than Words

The image of Germany's premier Angela Merkel greeting France's Emmanuel Macron in an Indian namaste spoke volumes of the impact of Covid-19 in the world. The Afghan girl's image on the cover of *National Geographic* magazine in 1984 perhaps caused more awareness and curiosity about the state of Afghan refugees than any other event that year or in that decade. The global environmental organization Greenpeace successfully used stark imagery to tell a powerful story about climate change in the 2000s. Their staff protested against alleged climate offenders, in public places, wearing life-like animal suits. The bottomline is that images communicate more than just words. Not just still photographs, videos, memes and GIFs can convey a powerful story.

As more people, especially first-generation smartphone users, consume content online, photo-sharing and video-sharing platforms have evolved into powerful conveyers of messages. Today, technology and fintech startups in South Asia spend millions of dollars to reach new and niche users via video-sharing platforms.

While world and societal events may give us powerful images of human achievements and endurance, the most powerful images in the corporate world are not arrived at serendipitously. A lot of planning goes into creating a powerful image that coveys what your brand or organization wants to convey. Also, these images may not be limited to still photographs. The global iPhone launches, the 'How dare you' speech[1] by Greta Thunberg in 2019 and the Madhya Pradesh government's 'Hindustan ka Dil Dekho' bioscope video[2] are examples of powerful imagery that can change the narrative or develop it.

Moments Create Energy

You think you are the most innovative company in your space. You have a technology or business model that no one else does. You think your users should care about it. Well, they don't! Unless you are operating in a narrow niche and solving one specific user problem, for example, Whatsapp in its early avatar. Then you can survive on the back of your engineering smarts and easy user experience. Most brands and organizations need to tell their story to attract users. Creating appropriate 'moments', or specific points in time, to convey a well-crafted message to a wide audience helps establish your brand message. These moments may be dictated by product or business milestones or determined by extraneous circumstances such as a regulatory policy change.

Creating a specific 'moment', when all your various audiences are focused on listening to what you say, is an important part of communicating your brand message. Mobile phone companies do it well during their product launches. Glitzy events that get amplified to millions of users via online platforms have become the hallmark of a phone launch. They also generate energy in the supply and distribution ecosystem. They excite investors and shareholders. It perhaps started with the first iPhone launch[3] in 2007. Before that, Microsoft did it for their Windows product launches. The Windows 95 product launch was a much-documented 'moment'.

The moment may not be a high-budget glitzy event that is widely televised. It may be a small, intimate event for a small group of influencers who can then amplify the story for your brand.

This brings us to the next element of communications: Allies.

Allies Lend Credence and Help Create Belief

Allies are people, groups of people or organizations, that help you communicate with your audiences. These may be your industry peers, industry associations, analysts or senior media editors – people and organizations that your audiences trust and believe in.

Brands use sportspeople, movie stars or political/constitutional heads as allies to deliver their messaging. In the online world, video-sharing platform celebrities, for example, YouTube stars, are commonly roped in for these purposes. Talk show hosts and standup comedians are a new genre of allies that organizations are experimenting with. A deliberate approach to co-opt allies for your communication is important for creating a successful communications outreach.

Stories Anchor Your Communications

The above four elements of communications come together and are anchored in the story: the narrative. The story needs to answer all your audiences' questions about why, what, when, where and how. It also needs to answer the question, 'What's in it for me?' Stories may be in the form 2000-word text articles or jazzy video stories, or just a plain chat between two people (voices for your brand). The format may depend on who your audience is and what is their preferred form of consuming information. The story should tell your audience why they should care about your product, your service or your message.

In recognition of how important stories are, many global and local brands now run first-party storytelling platforms as an integral part of their owned digital assets. Microsoft News

Center, Flipkart Stories, Mahindra's Rise are examples of such platforms.

Bringing together the five elements in perfect balance is the job of an expert communicator. When you bring these five elements together, well, you will have created an excellent perception-building framework.

14

BUILDING A STRONG COMMUNICATIONS DEPARTMENT

BUILDING A COMMUNICATIONS TEAM can be complex, much like any other management function in an organization. With the evolving nature of the function you have many pools of talent to choose from and several different areas that you can invest in – branding expertise, editorial writing, storytelling, video production, media relations, social media sentiment analysis, data analysis, community relations – the list is a long one. It is important to start with what you need the communications team to deliver for your brand. After that, hire the people with relevant skills and experience. Then arm the team with the support and resources they need to do their jobs well.

Hiring the Right Team

There are a few specific attitudes and leadership qualities that are more important than others when building a communications team.

1. **Maturity:** We consider maturity the most important quality in a good communications professional. Maturity lies in correctly understanding and assessing the position of the brand vis-à-vis its competitors and industry peers, and in devising ways in which the brand should respond to ongoing conversations in the industry. Maturity is also about being able to develop a point of view that is fair and balanced and keeps both the brand's as well as all stakeholders' interests in mind. For example, if you run an IT company that uses artificial intelligence, it is important to have a clear point of view about whether artificial intelligence is good for humanity or not. Sure, millions of dollars of your own revenue depend on using artificial intelligence-based products and services, but industry analysts are consistently highlighting the misuse of artificial intelligence. In such a scenario, you should be able to state your point of view honestly and authentically, without eroding organizational impact. A mature communications team can help in the nuanced articulation of the CEO's view. Teams with high maturity also have the confidence to experiment with new ideas. They are not afraid to fail in the short term and learn from their mistakes.

2. **Handling ambiguity:** Change is indeed the new normal in the world. Working through a developing business or customer situation is an important part of a communications team's job. Communications teams

are constantly dealing with changing business, market and cultural environments. They must create balanced messages that their organization can deliver to their stakeholders. Often the messaging needs to reassure the audience. The team also needs to be able to look around corners and anticipate future change. Such situations may be related to a government or regulatory policy change, a new audience sentiment or an emerging fashion trend. Communications teams should be able to prepare the organization for situations that may develop over a matter of days, weeks or months.

3. **Integrity:** Integrity is important in every job, but in communications it can be the difference in building brand value or eroding it. Organizations and brands face many communications dilemmas. For example, how much should you disclose when your database has been hacked into and customer data has been compromised? Or, if an employee has alleged wrongdoing in the workplace, should you discuss the incident in public? A communications team that has a strong sense of what is right and wrong, can deliver a balanced message.

4. **Focus on Execution:** Let's think in terms of doers versus thinkers. Do you have a good mix of doers and thinkers in the team? Is that brilliant strategist able to break the strategy down into small tasks for execution? Or does a plan remain just a plan? Does the team execute with speed and quality?

Internal Team or External Agency

Should you invest in creating a communications department within the company or outsource it to an agency? There are several examples of brands that build all capabilities in-house. Paisa Bazaar is one such brand in India.

I (Gayatri Rath) worked in three branding and communications consultancies for seven years supporting large brands. Then I worked for three large brands as their in-house brand and communications head. Here's what I have learnt. If you are a complex business, focused on many different customer categories and with multiple products, you have most likely created a complex web of functions and outreach mechanisms to address your various audiences. An in-house communications team can connect the dots and synthesize the effort, align external experts and agencies, which can then deliver on your communications mandate.

Communications During Crisis

A crisis demands fast, proactive, and authentic communication. More so if the crisis involves lives or livelihood. Any crisis management team is incomplete without communications experts. However, it is foolish to expect communications experts to find a solution to everything the company faces in a crisis. Communications people must work closely with other experts within an organization to respond to a crisis. It is also impractical for professionals to kill negative stories about a brand during a crisis. What they can do, however, is help CEOs respond to criticism in an authentic, empathetic manner. They can also organize the facts, build context and plan disclosures that can present the company's or brand's point of view transparently, thus keeping 'brand trust' intact.

Empowering the Team to Deliver

Empowering the communications team to deliver is an important part of achieving an organization's communications agenda. If the majority responses to the following questions are yes, your communications team is empowered:

1. As CEO, do you help your communications team understand what your priorities are? Have you shared with them your vision of what the team should deliver? Have you found out if the communications leader's vision is aligned with your idea of success?
2. Do you invite the communications team to business meetings and give them an opportunity to understand the business challenges and opportunities you and the leadership team are facing?
3. As CEO, do you review the team's plans and give feedback to improve such plans and align them better with business goals?
4. Do you ask for their opinion and take their feedback seriously?
5. Do they feel confident to do the right thing in every situation even though it may sometimes mean going against the personal opinion or preference of a leadership team member?

Building a communications function is a long-term commitment. Organizations must not focus on short bursts – during a crisis or a funding round. You don't start knitting a sweater just as it starts snowing. You also don't start building a stormwater drain when there is forecast of torrential rains later in the week. Communications for brand building requires many years of investments, planning and execution.

ANNEXURES

Annexure 1

HISTORY OF THE PRESS RELEASE

THE PRESS RELEASE FIRST originated in 1906, after a train wreck in New Jersey which caused the death of over fifty people. At the time of the accident, the train was owned by the Pennsylvania Railroad, it's publicity officer Ivy Lee[1], convinced his firm to issue a statement to outline what had happened. As the story has it, the account was printed verbatim by the *New York Times*.[2]

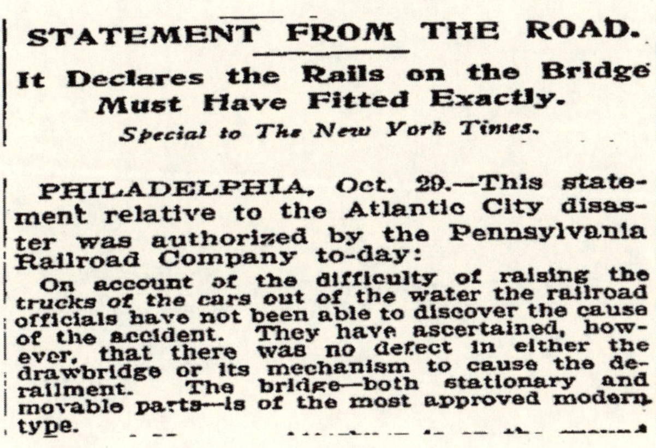

STATEMENT FROM THE ROAD.

It Declares the Rails on the Bridge Must Have Fitted Exactly.

Special to The New York Times.

PHILADELPHIA, Oct. 29.—This statement relative to the Atlantic City disaster was authorized by the Pennsylvania Railroad Company to-day:

On account of the difficulty of raising the trucks of the cars out of the water the railroad officials have not been able to discover the cause of the accident. They have ascertained, however, that there was no defect in either the drawbridge or its mechanism to cause the derailment. The bridge—both stationary and movable parts—is of the most approved modern type.

Over a hundred years later, there are many versions of the press release in circulation: digital release, multimedia release and video news release. In 2013, Amazon turned this on its head by tweeting fourteen posts announcing the launch of its latest version of the Kindle reader.

Is the press release dead? No. It is still the most reliable and credible source of information about a firm. In spite of the regular call for its demise, it still forms the heart of basic business communication aimed at mass media.

Annexure 2

PRESS RELEASE DO'S AND DON'T'S

Action	Impact	Option
Issue the release with the company logo.	Shows that it's an official communique of the company.	Include more information in a background note without a logo to show that it is not an official company statement but extra information.
Keep it short and sweet. One page is ideal, no more than two.	A short release will hold the reporter's attention better.	Include an editor's note to focus the attention of the journalist, in case it's a long release.
Let the spokesperson's quote flow organically in the copy; avoid ending with a quote.	An organically fitted quote has a better chance of being picked up.	End the release with a quote that takes the story forward.

Action	Impact	Option
The quote is for opinion, copy for the fact.	A quote is meant to add perspective to existing facts, not repeat facts that have been already mentioned in the copy. A perspective or an insight-based quote has a greater chance of being carried.	Use numbers, technical information and a quote only if it's very startling and needs the spokesperson's weight to verify it.
Don't change dates of releases and resend.	The journalist will think you are unethical and dishonest for pretending the release is the latest.	Update the release with new information: a fresh quote, region-specific facts. If you can't do that, write a pitch note of five lines and include the release as background without changing the date.
One size doesn't fit all.	A release for the business media will need to have that focus, for a tech product a different focus and a different one if it is food.	You can easily reformat your releases by changing the top half with an audience specific focus.
Include pictures, media links and video links	The media, especially digital media, expect all material in one handy guide: the press release. It becomes the source for all multimedia channels.	Really no option for this. At the very least a picture: logo, spokesperson or sector activity is a must.

Source: Paarul Chand

Annexure 3

EXCERPTS FROM CEO INTERVIEWS ABOUT COMMUNICATIONS

Ashish Gupta, former CEO, Docprime

'Corporate communications is important. What happens is there is a vision and today we may be only 40–50 per cent of that vision. So when we talk to our stakeholders, let's say we are talking to a large hospital or the laboratories, or we are talking to potential partners, do they understand how this ties up because looking at our website today, since it is not complete yet, you may not get the complete picture. The story has to reach out to anybody who could tomorrow become a part of this ecosystem ... so here is what it is, here is what we are trying to do in the next few years, and if you think the alignment works, then why don't you get in touch with us.

One of our PR narratives was that we are going to end up investing thirteen per cent of the funds available to us into preventive healthcare and OPD procedures, including dental. Now if you look at our website that may or may not be apparent, because you will see online consult as the largest piece. Which is true — online consult is our largest piece but that doesn't mean that our budgets aren't going to any other initiative. Those initiatives may become live and available to customers in the following months, but from a partner's perspective, if somebody wants to partner with us for preventive healthcare, the time to do it is now. So you see that bit of the dichotomy between what's available on the site and how a site would be perceived, versus what it is going to be shaping forward—this is where PR steps in. I can't do a television ad, I can't do a marketing ad talking about prevention because when customers look at it, and they come to the site and say "Hey, I don't see where you have advertised, where is it?" But PR can talk about it and that's when it becomes critical.'

Bhaskar Pramanik, former Member of the Board, State Bank of India and former Chairman of Microsoft Corporation India

'The role of the Board is primarily in the areas of governance, strategy, and leadership development. It is focused on the "what" of communications, especially to employees and stakeholders. Management is responsible for its execution.

The Board's role becomes more important in times of change – when the organization is seeking to transform itself from within or when it is forced to change because of external conditions.

At times of crisis like the current pandemic, the role of the Board becomes more pronounced. One of the musts of the Board is to ensure that the management has a clear communications plan for customers, employees, vendors and shareholders.'

D. Shivakumar, Group Executive President of Corporate Strategy and Business Development, Aditya Birla Management Corporation

'It is very important for the CEO to communicate with the organization regularly and also when there are special events or the media is speculating or saying something. Today's internal communications involves the CEO, the communications team and the HR director because of the sensitive nature of policies. The CEO has to orchestrate this ... The CEO and the communications team need to figure out the narrative clearly. Many communications teams try to protect the CEO from bad news or challenging questions and that's the worst thing The CEO cannot be protected in today's rich content world.'

Suresh Narayanan, Chairman and Managing Director, Nestlé India

'When you are up against [a] crisis of this kind, seldom [do] you come across functional problems (problem of a single function or department). It's very important that everybody in the organization comes together. But there are key people and key functions that perform an important role of communicating.

The purpose of every organization whether Nestlé or any other organization, brand, be it Maggi or otherwise evolves around two things that are the core of the organization. First of all is all of us at Nestlé as a company are seeking trust from our consumers. The trust is at the centre of [the] relationship between the consumer and the company.

Secondly, if you say that trust is the centre of relationship, if you say that, perception is reality, then it's important that you have to say what you mean and you have to mean what you say. Both of these are important. But in that sense in a normal situation the conversation is calmer, is at a less tense pitch and is more devoid of human views and is more straightforward. In a crisis the conversation gets lost because somebody is hurting. It's either the consumer who is hurting or doubting or the environment is hurting the company. So, the role of communication comes [at] that core point [during a] crisis. We have to communicate what is the purpose of the company. Nestle's purpose of ensuring healthier requirements for consumers wherever they are, it is a core value. What we do, our values rest around this point. There is respect for individuals and respect for each other.'

Vani Kola, Managing Director, Kalaari Capital

'Treat crisis as an opportunity and ensure maximum people should be productive, and how can we create more productivity for them. Can we develop new skills for people? Can you also make it the finest hour for each individual? Trust is the most important thing. Can you make this a deeper bonding with the company? If you can create that it would be the finest hour for the company.'

Vicky Bindra, chief product officer, FIS

'I actually think in a B2B company you can survive without marketing, you can't survive without communications. In a B2C company I think it has to co-exist with marketing so you have to have both. But the best companies are where they [bring them] together. So marketing and communications is one function because the umbrella is actually decided by communications and marketing becomes a subset.'

Annexure 4

COMMUNICATIONS MEASUREMENT TOOLS

This is an indicative list of firms and software tools that can help measure and assess the impact of communications programs and initiatives.

1. ClanConnect.ai: https://www.clanconnect.ai/
2. Cision: https://www.cision.com/us/
3. Meltwater: https://www.meltwater.com/en
4. YouGov: https://in.yougov.com/en-hi/
5. Germin8: https://www.germin8.com/
6. Sociabble: https://www.sociabble.com/
7. M Brain: https://www.m-brain.com/
8. Google Analytics: https://analytics.google.com/analytics/web/
9. RiskSTAT by RuderFinn: http://www.ruderfinn.com/
10. Impact Research and Measurement: https://impactmeasurement.co.in/
11. Business Fights Poverty: https://businessfightspoverty.org/

AUTHORS' NOTES

INDUSTRY PROFESSIONALS REFER TO the profession and function as communications or communication. We have used the term 'communications' in this book.

In certain cases, public relations (PR) and communications have been used interchangeably.

This book has been written by the authors based on their personal experiences and interpretations of public events as reported in mass media. Examples from personal experiences of each author (when presented in first person) have been clearly marked with the author's name whose experience it was.

Both authors live and work in India. As a result, a large number of examples and references are with respect to India-based organizations, events and personalities.

A few popular brand names have been referenced in the book. All references are in good faith and based on the authors' understanding of their relevance to the subject in discussion.

***

I feel fortunate to have experienced the beginning of the professional communications industry in South Asia in the 1990s. I and my peers were the first group of communicators who relied on the power of stories to do our jobs. Storytelling skills are different from those that were used by professionals before us – the power of relationships. That had earned it the sobriquet 'wine-and-dine' profession. (I can almost hear indignant exclamations from my seniors in the profession as I say that.) We were also a group of professionals who did not speak English with a British accent or write it like literature majors. We lived and worked through the rise of professional business journalism in the region. Our generation was also fortunate to experience the coming of the Internet and the fundamental changes it brought to communications and storytelling.

And yet, when I look around myself, so much has not changed. Many corporate leaders in South Asia still consider communications as it was a generation ago. Far too much emphasis on good English, personal relationships with editors in mainline mass media and too little emphasis on messaging, storytelling or audience targeting. Then there are organizations that hire communicators more to stop negative media stories than to tell positive ones. There is also the occasional example of the corporate communicator behaving as an additional executive assistant to the CEO.

In my opinion, communicators must take at least half of the blame for the undervaluation of a critical management function.

I have worked closely with over fifteen CEOs in half a

dozen big and small organizations. I think my experience is representative of the state of the profession in this part of the world. With this book, I hope we can start a conversation about recognizing communications as a serious profession that uses specific skills and tools to generate commercial value and to drive societal impact. The communications function brings a unique and rich perspective that can guide organizations through growth, change, and help build trust. I hope this book is just the beginning, and that many more people will find inspiration in it to write about this topic in the future.

Gayatri Rath

***

MY FIRST BRUSH WITH the world of communications was as a brash business and political reporter with TV18, now called Network 18. As a business reporter, PR professionals often fell in the category of carriers of press releases and invites from CII and FICCI, two of the biggest sources of early business news content in the 1990s. For the political reporter, professional PR executives did not really exist, as communications was handled entirely by the party spokesperson.

It took leaving active TV news and a foray into media advocacy for social sector issues for me to realize the deep value and impact of a well-crafted communications strategy. A decade of media advocacy and communications for issues of public health such as HIV/AIDS, TB and malaria as well issues of free and equal access to knowledge, led to a deeper understanding of how communication works. Working with the iconic Bachi Karkaria for a front-page story in the *Times of India* about the funding of the fight against HIV/AIDS was the pinnacle of understanding what smart communications can achieve for me. Managing communications for Wikipedia in India was a different experience altogether. Wikipedia is a truly transparent organization and very open with the media.

When the opportunity to lead India's first dedicated communications magazine came my way, I had understood enough about the potential of PR and the way it weaves into brand building and businesses to jump at the chance to go back to active journalism. I was fortunate to start PRmoment in India at a time when the communications profession was evolving and going far beyond media relations and was well into a series of international consolidations.

Post Covid-19, communications is seeing a major shift once again. Once again, like many other industries at the moment, PR has been propelled to handle a complex business, technological and social environment. As life and work change irrecoverably, what has not changed is the very human need to communicate, as new ways and methods are being evolved to deal with online communication. For the first time, communication is being discussed at the board level. Like a life-giving river on the banks of which great civilizations flourish, the modern corporate communications department is fast becoming the nerve centre of modern business, a great tool that all CEOs should institutionalize and use.

Paarul Chand

ACKNOWLEDGEMENTS

WE ARE GRATEFUL TO the many CEOs, business leaders and senior communications professionals who have contributed to this book with their personal experiences and advice.

Thanks are owed to:

Amandeep Arora, Head of Corporate PR, she has handled communications for Docprime, Policybazaar and Paisabazaar.

Ambereen Ali Shah, Head of Media Relations, Nestlé in India.

Anindita Phukan, a seasoned communications professional at Microsoft India, who was formerly with Nokia India.

Ashish Gupta, former CEO, Docprime.

Bhaskar Pramanik, former Member of the Board, State Bank of India and former Chairman of Microsoft India. He was also the CEO of Sun Microsystems in India for fourteen years.

Billy Vaughan, Managing Partner at Diversity Training University International, US, is an expert in diversity and inclusion practices and processes in the US and other geographies.

Dave Samson, former General Manager of Public Affairs, Chevron and part of Hall of Fame, Arthur W. Page Society, US.

D. Shivakumar, Group Executive President of Corporate Strategy and Business Development, Aditya Birla Management Corporation, and former CEO of Pepsi Co India and Nokia India.

Debjani Ghosh, President, NASSCOM for her support and for writing the foreword to this book.

Kavita Doshi at NASSCOM's communications team.

Madan Bahal, Co-founder and Managing Director of Adfactors PR, for his support.

Nandhita Nandakumar of Kaalari Capital.

Nirmala Menon, Founder and CEO of Interweave Consulting India, who has worked in the diversity and inclusion area in India for over twenty years.

Richard Edelman, Chairman and CEO of Edelman, for his valuable inputs, and the Edelman team, for generously sharing background information from the Edelman Trust Barometer studies.

Sanjay Khajuria, the Director of Corporate Affairs, Nestlé India, who has been at the forefront of corporate affairs at Nestlé India for over a decade after spending more than a decade in the company's legal function.

Suresh Narayanan, Chairman and Managing Director of Nestlé India is a people-oriented business leader and has led business operations in many different countries before returning to India to lead Nestlé.

Vani Kola, Managing Director of Kalaari Capital, for answering our questions about leadership in times of crisis.

Vicky Bindra, the Chief Product Officer at FIS, who has formerly worked with Pine Labs, Visa, MasterCard and GE Capital.

This book would not have been published without the support and encouragement of our families, friends and well-wishers.

We want to specially thank Sohini Bhattacharya who guided us through this project in her quiet, indomitable way. We are grateful for your support.

Gayatri Rath would like to thank her family. Pravin and Aryaman were patient supporters through the two years leading up to the book. She is grateful to Ravi Narayan, Rita Pani and Rajat Agrawal who went out of their way to introduce the authors to certain CEOs. She would also like to thank Ila Chhabra, Geetika Arora, Tithi Sarkar and Anissha Aggarwal, for their constant encouragement.

Paarul Chand would like to thank her Mom, Dad, Nani and Nikhil for their unstinting support for this book. She would also like to thank PRmoment India publisher and Incite Publishing CEO, Ben Smith, for his support for this book.

A very special thanks to our literary agent Mita Kapur at Siyahi. Without her guidance and support this book would have lain dormant in various files. Many, many thanks to our editors at Pan Macmillan India for believing in two unknown authors and giving wings to our very first book.

Last but not the least, the four-legged, often upside-down, furry cheerleader Linus, always ready with wags and licks of support during rewrites.

NOTES

Introduction

1. Chand, Paarul. 'Advantage Modi: the Success of the Enrage and Engage Communication Strategy.' PRmoment.in, 22 May 2019. https://www.prmoment.in/pr-insight/advantage-modi-the-success-of-the-enrage-and-engage-communication-strategy.
2. Dishman, Lydia. '3 Must-Have Traits for Courageous Leadership in a Post-Pandemic Workplace.' *Fast Company*, 28 May 2020. https://www.fastcompany.com/90509920/3-must-have-traits-for-courageous-leadership-in-a-post-pandemic-workplace.
3. Collins, Jim. 'The Misguided Mix-up of Celebrity and Leadership.' Accessed 9 October 2020. https://www.jimcollins.com/article_topics/articles/the-misguided-mixup.html.

1. Rise of the Corporate Communications Department

1. '1950s: Dealer-Automaker Relations.' NADA. Accessed 10 October 2020. https://www.nada.org/1950s/.
2. The authors interviewed Dave Sampson in October 2018.
3. Clifford, Stephanie. 'Video Prank at Domino's Taints Brand.' The New York Times. The New York Times, 16 April 2009. https://www.nytimes.com/2009/04/16/business/media/16dominos.html.

4. Armonk. 'MEDIA ALERT: IBM Expands Its Virtual Worlds Initiatives With a First-of-Its-Kind Virtual Block Party in Second Life.' IBM News Room, 10 October 2006. https://www-03.ibm.com/press/us/en/pressrelease/20411.wss.
5. 'Second Life.' Wikipedia. Wikimedia Foundation. Accessed 20 September 2020. https://en.wikipedia.org/wiki/Second_Life.
6. Gupta, Surajeet Das. 'How India Became Pepsi's Right Choice.' *Business Standard*, 27 March 2014. https://www.business-standard.com/article/companies/how-india-became-pepsi-s-right-choice-114032701308_1.html.
7. PTI. 'Internet Users in India to Reach 627 Million in 2019: Report.' *Economic Times*, 6 March 2019. https://economictimes.indiatimes.com/tech/Internet/Internet-users-in-india-to-reach-627-million-in-2019-report/articleshow/68288868.cms.
8. Kotler, Philip, Hermawan Kartajaya and Iwan Setiawan. *Marketing 4.0: Moving from Traditional to Digital*. Hoboken, NJ: Wiley, 2017.
9. Global communications consultancy Edelman runs an annual survey called Edelman Trust Barometer which is a global communications best practice. Organizations may, however, define their own trust barometers.

2. Communications or Marketing?

1. 'About.' Microsoft. Accessed 10 October 2020. https://www.microsoft.com/en-us/about.
2. Bishop, Todd. 'Exclusive: Satya Nadella Reveals Microsoft's New Mission Statement, Sees "Tough Choices" Ahead.' *GeekWire*, 25 June 2015. https://www.geekwire.com/2015/exclusive-satya-nadella-reveals-microsofts-new-mission-statement-sees-more-tough-choices-ahead/.
3. Ries, Al and Laura Ries. *The Fall of Advertising and the Rise of PR*. BusinessNews Publishing, 2014.

4. Ries, Al and Laura Ries. *The Fall of Advertising and the Rise of PR*. BusinessNews Publishing, 2014.
5. 'Stories from the World of GE.' GE News. Accessed 10 October 2020. https://www.ge.com/news/.
6. 'Home.' Microsoft News Center India. Accessed 10 October 2020. https://news.microsoft.com/en-in/.
7. 'Are You Looking for a Flipkart Story?' Flipkart Stories, 7 October 2020. https://stories.flipkart.com/.
8. 'Business Roundtable Redefines the Purpose of a Corporation to Promote "An Economy That Serves All Americans".' Business Roundtable, 19 August 2019. https://www.businessroundtable.org/business-roundtable-redefines-the-purpose-of-a-corporation-to-promote-an-economy-that-serves-all-americans.

3. CEO's Role #1: Listen Well

1. Sharp, Nathan. 'It's Facebook Official, Dating Is Here.' About Facebook, 5 September 2019. https://about.fb.com/news/2019/09/facebook-dating/.
2. The authors spoke with Nestlé India executives in late 2018 in preparation for this book.
3. 'Alan Turing.' Wikipedia. Wikimedia Foundation. Accessed 22 September 2020. https://en.wikipedia.org/wiki/Alan_Turing.
4. Gayatri Rath was an employee of Microsoft India between 2013 and 2018.

4. CEO's Role #2: Message Clearly

1. The authors spoke with Vani Kola in October 2020.
2. Vijay Govindarajan, Anup Srivastava and Luminita Enache. 'Understanding India's Chilly Reception of Jeff Bezos.' Harvard Business Review, 23 January 2020. https://hbr.org/2020/01/understanding-indias-chilly-reception-of-jeff-bezos.

3. Tata, Ratan (@RNTata2000). Twitter. Accessed on 10 October 2020. https://twitter.com/RNTata2000?lang=en.
4. Chand, Paarul. 'Former CNBC TV 18 Journalist Ankit Vengurlekar to Lead PR and Communications at Xiaomi India.' PRmoment. in, October 7, 2019. Accessed on 10 October 2020. https://www.prmoment.in/pr-news/former-cnbc-tv-18-journalist-ankit-vengurlekar-to-lead-pr-and-communications-at-xiaomi-india.
5. PK, Jayadevan. 'Flipkart's Sachin and Binny Bansal Turn into Delivery Men for Smartphones .' ETBrandEquity.com, 16 October 2015. https://brandequity.economictimes.indiatimes.com/news/marketing/flipkarts-sachin-and-binny-bansal-turn-into-delivery-men-for-smartphones/49401277.
6. An interview with Paarul Chand.

5. CEO's Role #3: Drive Branding

1. 'Five Reasons Why CEO Vishal Sikka Had to Leave Infosys.' *The Economic Times*. Economic Times, 18 August 2017. https://economictimes.indiatimes.com/tech/ites/five-reasons-why-ceo-vishal-sikka-had-to-leave-infosys/articleshow/60114080.cms.
2. '#MeToo Movement: Flipkart's Binny Bansal Quits over Serious Personal Misconduct' Charges.' Mumbai Mirror. Mumbai Mirror, 13 November 2018. https://mumbaimirror.indiatimes.com/news/india/metoo-movement-flipkarts-binny-bansal-quits-over-serious-personal-misconduct-charges/articleshow/66609075.cms.
3. Bezos, Jeff. 'No Thank You, Mr. Pecker.' *Medium*. Medium, 8 February 2019. https://medium.com/@jeffreypbezos/no-thank-you-mr-pecker-146e3922310f.
4. 'Our Story: Virgin.' Virgin.com. Accessed 10 October 2020. https://www.virgin.com/virgingroup/ content/our-brand-0.
5. Goyal, Deepinder. 'For Everything Else, Please Read the Performance Report Here' Twitter. Twitter, 10 July 2020. https://twitter.com/deepigoyal/status/1281550672106647552.

6. Agrawal, Soniya, Bradley Hope, Shekhar Gupta and Bismee Taskin. 'Customer Cancels Zomato Order over Muslim Delivery Boy, Company's Reply Wins Internet.' *The Print*, 31 July 2019. https://theprint.in/india/customer-cancels-zomato-order-over-muslim-delivery-boy-companys-reply-wins-Internet/270512/.
7. Chand, Paarul. 'Albinder Dhindsa, CEO of Grofers on What CEOs Want from Communicators.' PRmoment.in. Accessed 10 October 2020. https://www.prmoment.in/opinion/albinder-dhindsa-ceo-of-grofers-on-what-ceos-want-from-communicators.
8. Source: Gayatri Rath

6. CEO's Role #4: Be a Good Spokesperson

1. 'Business Roundtable CEOs Are Responding to Covid-19.' Accessed 11 October 2020. https://www.businessroundtable.org/Covid-19.
2. 'Amid Cautious Business Sentiment, China & India Most Likely to Lead Global Economic Recovery, Says India Inc.' *ET Insights*, 15 April 2020. https://etinsights.et-edge.com/amid-cautious-business-sentiment-china-india-most-likely-to-lead-global-economic-recovery-says-india-inc/.
3. Gurnani, C. P. 'An Indian IT Veteran's Tips for Corporate Leaders to Survive the Pandemic.' *Quartz India*. Quartz, 11 June 2020. https://qz.com/india/1863666/tech-mahindra-heads-tips-for-indian-ceos-to-tide-over-Covid-19/.
4. 'Coronavirus: Read Microsoft CEO Satya Nadella's Email to Employees.' *The Times of India*. Accessed 11 October 2020. https://timesofindia.indiatimes.com/gadgets-news/coronavirus-read-microsoft-ceo-satya-nadellas-email-to-employees/articleshow/74769780.cms.

5. Sharma, Unnati. 'Anand Mahindra Steps in to Help MP Boy Whose Father Cycled 106km to Get Him to Exam Centre.' *ThePrint*, 21 August 2020. https://theprint.in/india/anand-mahindra-steps-in-to-help-mp-boy-whose-father-cycled-106km-to-get-him-to-exam-centre/486682/.
6. Daga, Rashmi. 'Data Security Update.' Accessed 11 October 2020. https://www.freshmenu.com/data-security-update.
7. Kaur, Nehmat. 'How Brahminical Patriarchy Smashed Twitter.' *The Wire*, 21 November 2018. https://thewire.in/caste/should-twitter-smash-the-brahminical-patriarchy.
8. '2019 Edelman Trust Barometer: Executive Summary.' Accessed 11 October 2020. https://www.edelman.com/sites/g/files/aatuss191/files/2019-02/2019_Edelman_Trust_Barometer_Executive_Summary.pdf.
9. Scroll. 'Coronavirus: Swiggy to Lay off 1,100 Employees as Outbreak Hits Food Orders.' *Scroll*. Scroll.in, 18 May 2020. https://scroll.in/latest/962278/coronavirus-swiggy-to-lay-off-1100-employees-as-outbreak-hits-food-orders.
10. 'Coronavirus: Zomato to Lay off 13% of Its Staff, up to 50% Salary Cut for Other Employees.' *Scroll*. Scroll.in, 15 May 2020. https://scroll.in/latest/962048/coronavirus-zomato-to-lay-off-13-of-its-staff-up-to-50-salary-cut-for-other-employees.
11. 'Layoffs during Pandemic Shows India Inc's Lack of Empathy: Ratan Tata.' *Business Standard*, 23 July 2020. https://www.business-standard.com/article/companies/layoffs-during-pandemic-shows-india-inc-s-lack-of-empathy-ratan-tata-120072301738_1.html.

7. CEO's Role #5: Be Inclusive

1. 'PayPal Global – All Countries and Markets.' PayPal. Accessed 11 October 2020. https://www.paypal.com/uk/webapps/mpp/country-worldwide.

2. 'Where Is Coca-Cola Sold?: FAQ: Coca-Cola GB.' Coca. Accessed 11 October 2020. https://www.coca-colaafrica.com/packages/how-many-countries-sell-coca-cola-is-there-anywhere-in-the-world-that-doesnt.
3. Carr, Evan W., Andrew Reece, Gabriella Rosen Kellerman, and Alexi Robichaux. 'The Value of Belonging at Work.' Harvard Business Review, 16 December 2019. https://hbr.org/2019/12/the-value-of-belonging-at-work.
4. 'The People Experience Platform.' *BetterUp*. Accessed October 11, 2020. https://www.betterup.com/.
5. From an interview with the authors.
6. Smith, Michael. 'Xbox One Female Friendly Controllers.' Guardian Liberty Voice, 14 August 2016. https://guardianlv.com/2013/11/xbox-one-female-friendly-controllers/.
7. 'Micro-Inequity.' Wikipedia. Wikimedia Foundation. Accessed 14 July 2020. https://en.wikipedia.org/wiki/Micro-inequity.
8. 'Microaggression.' Wikipedia. Wikimedia Foundation, 7 October 2020. https://en.wikipedia.org/wiki/Microaggression.
9. Nadella, Satya, Greg Shaw, Jill Tracie Nichols, and Bill Gates. *Hit Refresh: the Quest to Rediscover Microsoft's Soul and Imagine a Better Future for Everyone.* New York: Harper Business, 2019.
10. Sams, Brad. 'Nadella: "I Answered That Question Completely Wrong".' Neowin, 10 October 2014. https://www.neowin.net/news/nadella-i-answered-that-question-completely-wrong.
11. One of the authors experienced this while was a Microsoft employee in India at that time.
12. 'Anand Mahindra Tweets about Inclusion.' *The Hindu*. The Hindu, 11 September 2018. https://www.thehindu.com/news/cities/mumbai/anand-mahindra-tweets-about-inclusion/article24929500.ece.
13. 'Tech Mahindra Fires Woman Accused of Bigotry, Homophobia by Former Employee.' The News Minute, 17 September 2018. https://

www.thenewsminute.com/article/tech-mahindra-fires-woman-accused-bigotry-homophobia-former-employee-88464.

14. Intersectionality refers to the intersection of different kinds of diversity e.g. historically, economically disadvantaged community within a religious minority. It is a complex and emerging subject and is beginning to show up in discussions about building inclusive corporate cultures.

8. The Covid-19 CEO and the Evolution of Communications

1. DeFilippis, Evan, Stephen Michael Impink, Madison Singell, Jeffrey T Polzer and Raffaella Sadun. 'Collaborating During Coronavirus: The Impact of Covid-19 on the Nature of Work.' NBER, July 30, 2020. https://www.nber.org/papers/w27612.
2. 'New York Covid-19 Map and Case Count.' *The New York Times*, 1 April 2020. https://www.nytimes.com/interactive/2020/us/new-york-coronavirus-cases.html.
3. Woodward, Ian C. 'Jacinda Ardern and Andrew Cuomo Are Crisis Comms Champions.' INSEAD Knowledge, 1 May 2020. https://knowledge.insead.edu/blog/insead-blog/jacinda-ardern-and-andrew-cuomo-are-crisis-comms-champions-14006.
4. Buckholtz, Alison. 'Lessons for Covid-19-era CEOs'. IFC, May 2020. https://www.ifc.org/wps/wcm/connect/news_ext_content/ifc_external_corporate_site/news and events/news/insights/Covid-19-era-ceo.
5. 'Rajiv Bajaj Has Four Posers for the Government on Lockdown.' *The Economic Times*. Accessed 11 October 2020. https://economictimes.indiatimes.com/news/economy/indicators/rajiv-bajaj-has-four-posers-for-the-government-on-lockdown/articleshow/76298284.cms.
6. 'United Colors of Benetton's Latest Campaign Celebrates Kindness.' ETBrandEquity.com, 27 August 2020. https://brandequity.

economictimes.indiatimes.com/news/marketing/united-colors-of-benettons-latest-campaign-celebrates-kindness/77778990.

9. Building Trust Circles

1. 'Nestle Seeks SC Nod to Destroy 550 Tonnes of Maggi Noodles.' *Business Standard*. Business-Standard, 21 September 2016. https://www.business-standard.com/article/companies/nestle-seeks-sc-nod-to-destroy-550-tonnes-of-maggi-noodles-116092101151_1.html.
2. 'Using Competitive Agility Index to Measure Trust in Business.' Accenture, 30 October 2018. https://www.accenture.com/us-en/insights/strategy/trust-in-business.
3. Climatebrad. 'BP CEO Tony Hayward: "I'd Like My Life Back",' YouTube video, 31 May 2010. https://www.youtube.com/watch?v=MTdKa9eWNFw& feature=youtu.be.

10. Managing Crisis

1. Paarul Chand
2. Paarul Chand's experience as the reporter
3. Deshpande, Salil. 'Why IndiGo Sacked the Man Who Filmed the Incident.' *Condé Nast Traveller India*. Condé Nast Traveller India, 8 November 2017. https://www.cntraveller.in/story/indigo-incident-really-happened-according-airline/.
4. 'IndiGo Skids 9% on Report of Rift between Promoters.' *The Economic Times*. Economic Times, 17 May 2019. https://economictimes.indiatimes.com/markets/stocks/news/indigo-skids-9-on-report-of-rift-between-promoters/articleshow/69367414.cms?from=mdr.
5. Yap, Chuin-Wei, Dan Strumpf, Dustin Volz, Kate O'Keeffe and Aruna Viswanatha. 'Huawei's Yearslong Rise Is Littered With

Accusations of Theft and Dubious Ethics.' *The Wall Street Journal*. Dow Jones & Company, 25 May 2019. https://www.wsj.com/articles/huaweis-yearslong-rise-is-littered-with-accusations-of-theft-and-dubious-ethics-11558756858.

6. Gupta, Surajeet Das. 'No Plan to Exclude Huawei, ZTE from 5G Infra Contracts: Sanjay Dhotre.' *Business Standard*. Business-Standard, 17 September 2020. https://www.business-standard.com/article/economy-policy/no-plan-to-exclude-huawei-zte-from-5g-infra-contracts-sanjay-dhotre-120091701553_1.html.
7. 'Donald Trump: US President Trump Says US Looking into Banning TikTok.' *Times of India*, 29 June 2020. https://timesofindia.indiatimes.com/world/us/trump-says-us-looking-into-banning-tiktok/articleshow/77247694.cms.
8. Vardharajan, Priyadarshini. 'TikTok Hits Hard after India Took Its Veil out: Bans Are Being Imposed All around the World Alarming a Security Threat.' Inventiva, 30 July 2020. https://www.inventiva.co.in/stories/priyadharshini/tiktok-hits-hard-after-india-took-its-veil-out-bans-are-being-imposed-all-around-the-world-alarming-a-security-threat/.
9. Reuters. 'TikTok CEO Says US Needs China-Owned App for Social Media Competition.' *NDTV Gadgets 360*. Gadgets 360, 29 July 2020. https://gadgets.ndtv.com/apps/news/tiktok-ceo-says-us-needs-china-owned-app-for-social-media-competition-2270944.

11. Measuring Impact

1. 'Disputes over Goodwill Can Seem Arcane.' *The Economist*. The Economist Newspaper. 30 August 2020. https://www.economist.com/business/2018/08/30/disputes-over-goodwill-can-seem-arcane.
2. Chand, Paarul. 'Data Driven Communications Is the Future: IBM's Ray Day at Chai Talk Special Events.' PRmoment.in, 22

November 2019. https://www.prmoment.in/pr-insight/data-driven-communications-is-the-future-ibms-ray-day-at-chai-talk-special-events.

12. Using the Right Tools

1. Robinson, Steve. 'What Is the PESO Model for Marketing?' Iterative Marketing, 15 November 2016. https://iterativemarketing.net/peso-model-marketing/.

13. The Five Elements of Communications

1. 'Greta Thunberg to World Leaders: "How Dare You? You Have Stolen My Dreams and My Childhood".' YouTube, 23 September 2019. https://www.youtube.com/watch?v=TMrtLsQbaok&feature=youtu.be.
2. 'Till Dekho Taad Dekho.' YouTube, 28 April 2020. https://www.youtube.com/watch?v=uRfQz6PCNMM&feature=youtu.be.
3. 'Steve Jobs Announcing the First iPhone in 2007.' YouTube, 8 October 2011. https://www.youtube.com/watch?v=wGoM_wVrwng.

Annexure 1: History of the Press Release

1. Gavin, Sarah. 'History of the Press Release' Outbrain Blog , 20 April 2020. https://www.outbrain.com/blog/history-of-the-press-release-gaining-value-from-tactics-new-and-old/.
2. 'The Importance of the Press Release.' Vela Agency, 25 September, 2020. https://velaagency.com/the-importance-of-the-press-release/.